IF YOU DON'T GO,
DON'T HINDER ME

THE ABRAHAM LINCOLN LECTURE SERIES
This series aims to reflect the principles that
Abraham Lincoln championed:
education, justice, tolerance, and union.

Bernice Johnson Reagon

IF YOU DON'T GO, DON'T HINDER ME

The African American Sacred Song Tradition

University of Nebraska Press, Lincoln and London

The lectures on which this
book is based were spon-
sored by the University of
Nebraska Press,
Athletic Department,
the College of Arts
and Sciences, College of
Fine and Performing Arts,
Teachers College, and
Office of Affirmative
Action and Diversity
Programs of the University
of Nebraska–Lincoln.
Library of Congress Cata-
loging-in-Publication Data
Reagon, Bernice Johnson,
1942–   If you don't go
don't hinder me : the African American sacred song
tradition/Bernice Johnson
Reagon.   p.   cm.—
(The Abraham Lincoln
lecture series) Includes
bibliographical references.
ISBN 0-8032-3913-0
(cloth : alk. paper)—
ISBN 0-8032-8983-9
(pbk.: alk. paper) 1. Gospel
music—History and criti-
cism. I. Title. II. Series.
ML3187 .R3187 2001
782.25'4—dc21
00-055231

N

To My Mother,
Beatrice Wise Johnson
1920–1999

Contents

Acknowledgments

Why would one for whom voice unleashed in air is the primary and strongest medium of presentation also move to the printed page? For me, it is because of the role of books in my life as a component of my survival. Reading was sacred to my life as an African American child and continues to be a major way for me to be able to create balance and solace in my life.

Going from live presentation to paper is excruciating for me and the journey is arduous and long. I actually have to translate my oral presentation—a "public-ation"—into what often feels like another language rather than another medium. I struggle to both respect the literary forum and at the same time push it to retain and unleash the sound of the original source, imprinted with the sound, nuance, and rhythm of my speaking voice. I am never satisfied, but as I am doing now, I let it go in an offering to you. I am indebted to the support community that circles around me to ensure I survive the process.

I am grateful to Nancy Rosen, who contacted me in 1996 about coming to the University of Nebraska–Lincoln to present a series of lectures on African American sacred music culture. I am also indebted to the University of Nebraska Press team who worked with the manuscript and moved it to its final stages.

My gratitude to ayodele ngozi and Adisa Douglas for their careful reading of the manuscript at several stages and for crucial recommendations that strengthened the clarity and order. Any resulting confusion and mutterings are mine by intentional choice.

Introduction

If You Don't Go, Don't Hinder Me. I am leaving this place. I would like company. If I have to travel alone, don't get in my way. The phrase I have selected as the title for this collection of essays is drawn from African American oral tradition. The text captures a kind of tension I wanted when I thought about a way of centering this series of presentations in African American sacred music culture. The essays are based both on my archival and field research as a scholar in the history of African American culture and on my personal biography as an African American woman coming of age as a cultural activist, musician, and composer.

Each essay is in some way about change and movement. "If You Don't Go, Don't Hinder Me," drawn from African American oral tradition, is much more than a phrase, it is also a song I have heard and sung all of my life:

If you don't go, don't hinder me
If you don't go, don't hinder me
If you don't go, don't hinder me
I'm on my way, great God, I'm on my way.

The text I have selected to name this collection is not in fact the first lines we would sing. First would come the overt declaration of leaving and going to another place:

I'm on my way to Canaan land
I'm on my way to Canaan land
I'm on my way to Canaan land `
I'm on my way, great God, I'm on my way.

With the verse about Canaan land, we are placed in the nineteenth century. Growing up in post–World War II Southwest Georgia, I heard stories that sometimes "Canaan" meant Canada, which is where many escaping slaves went after the 1850 Fugitive Slave Law was passed. This law legalized and obligated the active participation of the security forces of the local, state, and federal governments, along with the citizenry (ordinary citizens could be deputized to aid marshals in the line of duty) in effecting the return of fugitive slaves wherever they were found in the United States.

During the Civil Rights Movement of the 1960s, we sang this song but changed the word "Canaan" to freedom:

I'm on my way to freedom land
I'm on my way to freedom land
I'm on my way to freedom land
I'm on my way, great God, I'm on my way.

One word, "freedom," documents the time period. One would not have been able to sing freedom during the time when slavery was an integral part of this country. By the twentieth century, the 1960s, we had cleared enough space with our living and struggling and dying and going on that, no matter what, we could say and sing: "I want my freedom now!" When we sang this song during the sixties, we were talking about marching in our local communities, which might result in our arrest, leading to time in jail, beatings, or worse.

As campaigns challenging segregation and racism got underway in communities across the South, the decision to participate or not to participate was individual and personal, and a family and community matter. The decision had an impact on one's ability to continue to go to school, to hold a job, or to have housing. Pressure could also be placed on members of the family who were not directly involved. The decision to join the Movement brought out discussions and arguments with family and friends, and within church memberships, as to whether one should risk getting involved or not. In most cases those joining local protest activities (attending mass meetings, going to jail, marching) were in the minority. If the Movement gathered momentum, the numbers increased, and in several cases boycotts were effectively organized and sustained that required the active support of the entire African American community. This song clearly states that, "with a well made-up mind,"[1] the singing activists are committed to going forward no matter what.

During the Civil Rights Movement our freedom songs no longer operated in code. Whether you sang "freedom" during the sixties or the older traditional text with the word "Canaan," in essence the song says, I must leave or change where I am, and I want you to go with me:

> I asked my mother come and go with me
> I asked my mother come and go with me
> I asked my mother, come and go with me
> I'm on my way, great God, I'm on my way.

Brother, sister, pastor . . . I want you to go, but if you don't go, get out of my way:

If you don't go, going anyhow
If you don't go, going anyhow
If you don't go, going anyhow
I'm on my way, great God, I'm on my way.

If you don't go, don't hinder me. . . .

 During the nineteenth century, being on your way out of slavery usually meant leaving a place to go to another place, covering geographical territory. You actually had to put distance between where you were and where you were headed. During the twentieth-century Civil Rights Movement, being on your way often meant staying where you were and wreaking havoc in your local community, insisting on its transformation so that a new construction could be possible. Black people were determined to rearrange space for themselves and their future. We knew that as tax-paying citizens we deserved access to opportunities and resources provided by our organized governing bodies. It really was well overdue, this standing up and taking up new space – we had to move!

 Being born in the twentieth century, I learned this song in the nineteenth-century version with its reference to "Canaan" land. Twentieth-century "Canaan" in the stories and sermons of the Black Baptist churches I attended was about a life beyond this experience we were having on earth. It was different from the story about "Canaan" for the Hebrew children. That Canaan was a place on earth that was promised to them as a part of their covenant with their God – although they had to take it from the people who were there. What a strange way of giving.

 Anyway, when we sang this song and other songs about Canaan, we were talking about an "over yonder," an "up yonder," an afterlife – "across our Jordan River," on "the other side of death." Those stories and sermons held those songs for us until we began to fight against racism in this country and then the same songs, old songs, became new – lining up for use in the struggle, change a word here or there and there you have it – a freedom song, a new instrument for the struggle for freedom.

The Civil Rights Movement was about an internal and external moving. What you left when you joined the Movement were the old pacts you held within yourself to go along with racist, demeaning, unfair, inequitable policies that distorted your life and spirit. You did not leave town geographically, but in fact stayed and moved yourself through new behaviors and challenges, throwing your life up against a system and demanding that it fall so that something different could take its place.

During the first decades of the twentieth century, especially after the start of World War I, there was another kind of moving African Americans engaged in to change their lives. It was geographical. Moving from rural farming communities to urban centers of the nation, it was a massive migration taking place over the first four decades of the century and involved millions of people. Between 1915 and the 1940s, over fifteen million of us decided we had to make a geographical change and leave the place we knew as home and go somewhere else.

Why did so many of us feel we had to move? Slavery was gone, wasn't it? The abolition of slavery was secured with the Thirteenth Amendment, wasn't it? The Union victory – with the participation of thousands of Black soldiers – destroyed the infrastructure of the South, which had the enslavement of Black people as its lifeblood – the plantocracy was gone, wasn't it?

There is a story of triumph, terror, and betrayal that unfolds across the Southland between the time we call the year of Jubilee, which ended slavery, and the dawning of a new century that the historian Rayford Logan called the "nadir (the bottom, as low as you can go)."[2] We had over four million people changing status from slavery to freedom at the end of the Civil War. Four million Black people trying to figure out what it meant to be free in a devastated South. That in and of itself is a revolution. There were massive refugee efforts for Blacks and Whites who were displaced and destitute at the end of the war. For the first time in the South, the Reconstruction years brought schools for Black people and for Whites who could not afford to privately pay for their education.

The Fifteenth Amendment extended voting rights to Black men, and Southern states trying to be restored to the Union had to ratify it. In fact, had it not been for the requirement that former rebel states had to pass the Fifteenth Amendment, it would not have been ratified: several states north of the South were not in favor of Black enfranchisement.[3] That should have been a sign that these states were not sure they wanted the Black men of their communities to live among them as full voting citizens. Many in the North felt that with the end of the war they wanted to get on with a reconstructed nation in which business could expand. We should have known it would end, this fragile, inadequate effort to make democracy real for the South. But there was hope even in the face of danger, and the danger was real, because there were terrorist groups that began to form as soon as the Southern states began to be reorganized at the end of the war.

We were not all naive Black people walking into freedom during the latter part of the nineteenth century. Building our schools, building our churches, trying to find land to farm and jobs of any kind . . . and desperately reaching out – trying to find members of our families that had been sold away from us – we daily walked in danger. We had lived with these White people all our lives, and we knew how much they hated us free. But we worked, hoping that the federal troops would be enough to drive a wedge, so we could establish a different life beyond slavery that would make freedom available to us.

We died, some of us, as we built our communities under fire. The Reconstruction of the Union began to take place without our freedom at the center. In 1877 the federal troops were finally all gone, from Louisiana and South Carolina too. In a nationally disputed presidential election, the Republican Hayes was finally seated through a compromise, without our freedom and protection in mind, that promised to wipe away the notion of a Reconstruction. We would be left to those remnants of the Confederacy who had lost the war and lost slavery and wanted to rebuild the South, making sure that the place for Blacks would be properly controlled.

The South and the North got together again and, through federal policies from the congressional, executive, judicial, and military branches, actually expressed in deeds and legal statutes: "Do with your Black people what you will." We did not stop after the troops left. We kept teaching, building churches, reuniting our families, forming new families when we could not find our folk; we kept living unless we died. Kept trying to vote – the Black men, that is. And the terror became more organized, the terror became more random, became like the air. . . .

In the face of increasing terror bent on sending us back to slavery through new doors constructed in violence and fear with the sanction of too many, before the twentieth century dawned, many of us decided to leave. There was a movement called the

Exodusters, Black people who left old rebel states, especially Tennessee and Louisiana, moving to new territories in Kansas, Oklahoma, and Nebraska.[4] Black people moving in search of other spaces in this land of our birth, looking for a crack to force a space that would allow us to stand as tall as we sensed we could be.

Starting with the first decade of the new century, our leaving in massive numbers became known as the "Great Migration." We began, some of us, to leave the farms and rural communities and move to the towns, and from the towns to the cities. The promise of the city was that it was someplace else. The fresh air of the rural south was choking, stagnating, and binding because of racial, economic, social, and political oppression. The city had an openness, because we did not know it and it did not yet know us, it was untested and untried – uncharted ground. It had a kind of space that did not exist in small, farm-based communities. Its promise was that one could test one's abilities in a new land. In the wake of World War I, there was news that made us believe there were jobs, and we believed that we might be able to build something better for ourselves, our families, and our future. The need to find work that would pay a livable wage was and continues to be a phenomenon that creates extreme anxiety. If you are a slave, your labor is offered or forced in exchange for your life. If you are free, then somehow in a capitalist culture like the United States of America you have to find a way to turn your labor or whatever you have into funds – currency that will help you to support your life. And of course it took more than money. Moving was major, tearing, cataclysmic. Changes planned and unplanned, with hope for betterment, were almost always quite disruptive.

Leaving the plentiful land of the rural South to come to the cramped city so that we could have more space is a strange idea. Is it more territory? No indeed, there is much less geographical space. But Black people came to the city looking for more room. And the room was not horizontal, we wanted to move up and out. We wanted to somehow get somewhere where we could get a toe in, a foothold or fingerhook from which we could climb and pull us and ours up with and after us – spreading higher. We needed this new territory to transform our future. The need for change and larger opportunity was at the heart of the massive movement of African Americans to Chicago, New York, Birmingham, New Orleans, Cleveland, Washington, Boston, Memphis, Atlanta, Los Angeles, Philadelphia, and other urban centers during the first four decades of the twentieth century.

The journey from slavery to diminished freedom in the South to hitting the road any kind of way to someplace else was a long and winding and sometimes twisted journey. There was the issue of coming to a new place. Maybe you had family, maybe you did not, maybe you had a place to stay, maybe you had a chance of a job, maybe not – maybe you came wanting something better and found yourself in a strange new land with hesitancies in the welcome.

But move we did and the story of that moving changed the demographic lay of the land for those of us who left for new homes in new cities and those of who stayed to work out our existence in the communities of the South in which we were born. Migration as a theme looms large in twentieth-century African America. I have used it as a centering structure for four essays looking at different genres of sacred music as it manifested itself across the twentieth century and within my personal life.

How do you survive leaving everything you know to try to reconstruct your life and future in a new way? What do you carry with you on your journey to the new place? In this series of essays, I look at the place and function of our sacred music tradition as a source of strength that helped us to survive spiritually and emotionally in our new places within and without. When studied carefully, our music culture documents a lot about how we saw ourselves in our movings.

There is also an interesting and important story revealing how at various times we sought ways to use our most sacred musics, commodify that which was our soul's lifeblood, to assist us in extracting funding out of a system that was driven by possession, property, and commerce. This is not necessarily a statement of critique, but rather an acknowledgment of the dangerous roads we traveled as a people trying to make our way in this our native land.

There is the story of the evolution of gospel music looking at the work of Charles Albert Tindley, Thomas Andrew Dorsey, Rev. Smallwood Williams, Roberta Martin, Pearl Williams Jones, and Richard Smallwood. Then there is the story of Deacon William Reardon and the prayer bands that continued to carry the tradition of South Carolina spirituals through the twentieth century to the new locations of homes and churches in the communities of Washington DC and Baltimore. The concert spiritual tradition is the subject of an essay that is both about the tradition and how it was passed to me as an example of the way in which culture was transmitted from one generation to another through the education system created by African Americans in the final decades of the nineteenth century. The last essay explores the psychic territory of how stories about women from the nineteenth century became a constant source of strength and knowing for me as I came to myself as a young African American woman, singer, fighter, and scholar. It has also some of what it meant to move into my work under the shadow of a power and source like Bessie Jones, who seemed to remember so much of what she had been taught as a child and young adult growing up in Georgia. Here was a woman who was a singer, a storyteller, a healer, a believer of great faith, independent in the way she formed her ideas about womanhood, sexuality, and righteousness.

Today I do not know myself outside of these journeys, within the structures of transmission that include the culture into which I was born and nurtured and the constructed culture of education that trained me to be a scientist of culture. Here are glimmers of the partnerships I have tried to fashion out of all I have been given through my living.

Twentieth-Century Gospel

As the People Moved They Sang a New Song

I joined my first and only gospel choir when I joined the church at eleven years of age. It was the first gospel choir at Mt. Early Baptist, a small rural church in Dougherty County pastored by my father, Rev. Jessie Johnson. My sister Fannie, who played the piano, organized the choir. It was 1954 – gospel was everywhere. Most of the Baptist and Pentecostal churches inside the city of Albany, the county seat of Dougherty, already had gospel choirs. However, the country churches were sometimes a decade behind the city churches.

We loved gospel music, and the coming of our own gospel choir, our own choir standing in white gospel robes (which my mother made), was so exciting! We learned our songs off the radio, and sometimes Fannie would order sheet music from the Chicago-based gospel publishing companies. Every Sunday morning the local radio station, WGPC, was reserved for Black gospel music. This is where we heard the latest hits on the radio. Mahalia Jackson was one of my favorite singers; the Five Blind Boys of Jackson, Mississippi, were my favorite quartet. I loved the music of the Roberta Martin Singers from Chicago, Illinois, and the Davis Sisters from Philadelphia, Pennsylvania. In addition to a gospel DJ playing the nationally renowned groups, Sunday morning was also the time when we heard local quartets, who presented fifteen-minute programs sponsored by funeral homes or a local store.

African American gospel music began as the exciting new congregational and composed sacred music in urban Pentecostal, Baptist, and some Methodist churches. The congregations of these churches were made up of people who had moved to the city from the rural South. By midcentury, gospel was completing a circle of sorts, as the old home country churches whose families had been impacted by migration to the north began to organize their gospel choirs.

With the formation of a gospel choir, Mt. Early was entering a gospel era that had by then been underway for most of the century. Having a choir that sang songs separated from the rest of the congregation, purchasing a piano, paying a musician, having a church building with a choir stand: these were big steps for small congregations that had been carrying on their worship services based on traditions formed in the nineteenth century. Making room for the new music and choir altered the worship services. In the rural churches and in rarer instances in urban churches, gospel was added to the worship services with the older style of singing being relegated to a brief opening in devotional services, prayer meetings, and baptisms.

During this same period, as I began to sing gospel, my Uncle Charlie Johnson, a great quartet bass singer, and my Aunt Dorothy and their children, my cousins, moved from across the road from where we lived in Dougherty County, right outside of Albany, Georgia, to Philadelphia. I still have strong memories of wanting our family to move with them, but my parents said no. So our family stayed in the South, as did most African Americans. My uncle and aunt moved to a strange city, but they moved with the support of members of my aunt's family members, who had moved to Philadelphia earlier. By this time Philadelphia had an old and large African American community whose twentieth-century expansion had been based on the Great Migration of the past four decades.

There were several levels to the African American community in Philadelphia. The free Black community dated back to before this country was formed as an independent nation. Sometimes, especially during the twentieth century, when we moved to the city, the older African American neighborhoods in these cities both welcomed and worried about being overrun by the large numbers of "country" Black folk arriving daily from the South. What to do with them? There was so much they did not know. We didn't talk right, we didn't dress right, our behavior was downhomey, country, and sometimes embarrassing. Too often our education was sparse or nonexistent. At best the old urban communities of Black people survived in a fragile economic, social, and political balance with the larger unsympathetic White community. What would they do with the millions of Black people pouring off the farms into the neighborhoods looking for room to grow in the decreasing spaces of the urban landscape? Sometimes the welcome was hesitant.

Leaving the land of the rural South to seek out expanded possibilities in urban centers that were more crowded than one could ever imagine, and receiving a sometimes chilly reception – from the city, from the weather, from those who looked as if they were your people – made for a harsh transition. The welcome could be as cold as the wind coming over Lake Michigan into Chicago, and you would find yourself wondering whether this was the worst decision you'd ever made.

One of the founding fathers of the earliest form of composed gospel music, the gospel hymn, was a Methodist minister serving a congregation in Philadelphia as the stream of migrants from the South became a flood. Charles Albert Tindley was a minister who still remembered what it was like to have to leave. He had come to Philadelphia in 1875 when he was around eighteen years old, newly married, in search of a place big enough for his potential. He had come to family, an aunt, his deceased mother's sister. Tindley's father, who had been a slave in Berlin, Maryland, married a free Black woman. When she died, the baby, Charles Albert, was raised by her sister and until he was nine grew up in a free Black family. When Tindley was nine, his father, now remarried, took him back and farmed him out to work on plantations. Tindley taught himself to read and joined the Methodist church in Berlin. He moved to Philadelphia, found work as a hod carrier for brick masons, and worked as the sexton taking care of his church. At night he studied for the ministry, and against the odds and opinions of many misbelievers he passed the exams and became an ordained Methodist minister.[1]

In 1902, Tindley became pastor of the congregation he would lead for the next thirty years. He still remembered what it was like to need to leave and try to make a different life for yourself. He welcomed these Black people coming largely from Eastern Shore Maryland into his congregation, and he established his ministry as a foundation for helping them to move successfully into the city and into urban life. Through his church, newly arrived migrants were led to night classes, given leads for work, and urged to use the church saving plans, which allowed them to save up for a down payment on their row houses.

Charles Albert Tindley's ministry reflected his understanding that his congregation was expanding and had to serve people moving at different levels as they adjusted to city life. He was an innovative pastor and a gifted preacher whose sermons were legend. In looking at the moving that Blacks did during this time, Tindley's story is a good place to start. Within his church new practices were evolving for a new urban people, and it was reflected on every level of his ministry. A strong part of Tindley's preaching rested on his ability to tell a story with a lesson accessible to everyone in the congregation, no matter what their education. He was also a songwriter who created new sacred songs, several of which have become classics in the gospel-hymn canon.

I was drawn to Tindley, not because of his work with a migrant congregation, but because of his work as a songwriter of new sacred songs in the early years of the twentieth century. I was to discover that to study gospel one had to study the Great Migration. I found that I could not study Tindley's music without looking at his ministry in the church that was named for him after it was rebuilt in 1924.

Tindley wrote his new gospel hymns as a way of extending and amplifying his sermons. In 1901, we find him copyrighting his first songs. We don't know when he wrote them; we know this is when he grouped them together and sent them to the copyright office. His songs were already making their way through the Black church community. In 1916 he published a songbook called *Songs of Paradise*, and in 1932 he published a collection of his sermons called *Book of Sermons*. What you have in a man like Tindley, a self-educated man, is a person who actually sees himself in the path of history and participated in documenting his journey. Black people loved his songs: these were songs he had written as a part of his sermons and were heard first from his pulpit.[2]

His most popular song, "Stand By Me," is the second most well-known hymn in Black Christendom, after "Precious Lord," the gospel hymn composed by Thomas Andrew Dorsey in 1932. It is an interesting song to look at because it shows how he spoke to his congregation. He used their way of talking to fashion his lyrics:

STAND BY ME

When the storms of life are raging, stand by me
When the storms of life are raging, stand by me
When the world is tossing me, like a ship upon the sea
Thou who rulest wind and water, stand by me.

In the midst of tribulation, stand by me
In the midst of tribulation, stand by me
When the host of hell assail, and my strength began to fail
Thou who never lost a battle, stand by me.

In the midst of faults and failures, stand by me
In the midst of faults and failures, stand by me
When I do the best I can, and my friends misunderstand
Thou who knowest all about me, stand by me.

In the midst of persecution, stand by me
In the midst of persecution, stand by me
When my foes in battle array, undertake to stop my way
Thou who saved Paul and Silas, stand by me.

When I'm growing old and feeble, stand by me
When I'm growing old and feeble, stand by me
When my life becomes a burden and I'm nearing chilly Jordan
Oh thou Lily of the Valley, stand by me.

The poetry created out of the "talk" of the "regular" folks is full of motion, because of the way Tindley handles the presence and naming of God. The actual term God, Jehovah, does not appear in the lines. As a poet Tindley wove a circle using the experiences of his life and the lives of his members as if to say, "This is where I am or will be and I want company. Not just any company, but in the case of life being like 'a ship on a raging sea,' I want my company to be the One who rules the elements. When I am challenged and when I am persecuted and my enemies began to circle around me for the kill, I want standing with me the One who has never lost a battle, the One who was able to get Paul and Silas out of jail."

Tindley would also preach about getting old and feeble. He believed in miracles, as shown in his composition "Leave It There":

> If your body suffers pain, and your health you can't regain,
> And your soul is almost sinking in despair,
> Jesus knows the pain you feel, He can cure and He can heal,
> Take your burden to the Lord and leave it there.

But Tindley would also look out on his congregation and face them with the fact that they would get old and die. There would come a time when the body itself would be the burden in need of laying down to rise no more. The last stanza begins, "When I'm growing old and feeble, stand by me"; this is repeated twice, then the third line, "When my life becomes a burden, and I'm crossing chilly Jordan"; then Tindley goes to nature, "Oh thou Lily of the Valley, stand by me."

The other factor in selecting this song is that it gives us a graphic example of how the oral tradition interfaced with the Western notion of composed music. Tindley copyrighted his songs and had them set to Western musical notation. His songs were transmitted orally and through the printed score. Black people did not like all of Tindley's songs, but when they did – songs like "Stand by Me," "We'll Understand It Better By and By," "The Storm Is Passing Over," "Nothing Between," "Someday" (the song we generally call "Beams of Heaven," the funeral song), "What Are They Doing in Heaven Today?" and "Leave It There," to name a few – they were embraced and offered out again in every style and configuration one could imagine.

Most of the time when we sang these songs, we did not acknowledge Tindley as composer, because the songs came to us via the oral tradition without Tindley's name being connected with it. The singer of a Tindley composition often sang the song as a church song and sometimes seemed to think it was of her or his own creation. This may seem fraudulent with our Western sense of copyright; however, within the African-based tradition it is understandable. Within the Black tradition, one is not really considered a singer until one has found one's own way of presenting a work. In a way, "Stand By Me" performed by harmonica virtuoso Elder Roma Wilson, the Five Blind Boys of Alabama, the Caravans, and the Violinaires are all original compositions based on the Tindley composition. They are singing Tindley's song transformed by their own creative interpretation, and in most cases they do not credit Tindley. We can go further and say that when the rhythm-and-blues singer Ben E. King sang his version of "Stand By Me" as a love song, he owes Tindley, whose song gave us the central phrase "stand by me" and another way of asking for support and company.

Charles Albert Tindley also copyrighted "I'll Overcome Some-day" in his first group of songs in 1901. Although the text of the verses and the melody are different, the chorus is the same text that becomes the theme song of the Civil Rights Movement some six decades later. There are those who credit Tindley with creating the original song, but there is some evidence that a church song, "I'll Be Alright," was a part of Methodist and Baptist congregational repertoire by the turn of the century. This means that Tindley, himself a composer, operating within the African American oral tradition, may have drawn from his traditional core as much as he gave to it.[3]

The lessons from the gospel hymns of Charles Albert Tindley are reflected in almost any migration story you find. The historian Allan Ballard, who was born in Philadelphia, found in his autobiographical history of the migration of his family that his father's people moved to Philadelphia from South Carolina. Ballard found that African Americans moved sometimes in an effort to improve their economic conditions. He also found that racial violence, especially lynchings, drove many people to leave a place of racially based terror.

People began to leave Abbeville County after the Phoenix riot. In 1898, while thousands of Italians, Jews, and Slavs were fleeing Europe for the United States, a local paper described another migration: "During the past week, three cars of Negroes have left Greenwood for lower Mississippi. These cars have carried away 45, 35, and 24 Negroes, respectively." But it still took several years before the community gathered itself together to go North. And it took several other developments – the arrival of the boll weevil that decimated the cotton fields, forcing people to abandon farming, the war that created jobs in industry in the North, and the availability of cheap railroad tickets – before the journey out of this bloodsoaked land could really begin.[4]

In 1916, the same year Tindley published *Songs of Paradise*, Thomas Andrew Dorsey, the man who some sixteen years later would write "Precious Lord" and become known as the father of gospel music, was a young man moving to Chicago from Atlanta, Georgia. Dorsey, who actually coined the term "gospel" for the new sacred music, said that as he began to compose he tried to write like Charles Albert Tindley. According to Joe Williams, manager and lead singer with the Harmonizing Four Quartet of Richmond, Virginia, a group that began in 1928, so great was his association with the new music spreading through many urban congregations that occasionally new songs written in this style would be called "dorseys."[5]

Thomas Dorsey was himself among the millions who moved during this time, moving first with his family from Villa Rica, Georgia, to Atlanta in 1908, and then moving from Atlanta to Chicago in 1916. Dorsey grew up in a musical, religious Baptist family. He learned shape-note singing from his father, and the organ from his mother. Shape-note singing was a practice that moved south during the nineteenth century to train congregations to read music scores. These scores used a different shape for each note on the scale with the syllables *do re me fa sol la ti do*. In Atlanta, he received his only additional formal music training from a music teacher.[6]

Young Dorsey was also influenced by an uncle who played blues. Dorsey was a top blues pianist in Atlanta by the time he decided to move to Chicago. The move was a part of his search and struggle to make a living as a musician. Dorsey says of the images of Chicago:

> Between the years of 1912 until about 1918 is when the great exodus from the South to the North began with my people. And anything that moved seemed to have a bearing on them, the train – you couldn't say much about automobiles, because they didn't have them. But there I wrote a skit about the folks from the backwoods who took the straight line – straight to Chicago. They felt that money grew on trees, eggs were made in a factory, and man could scratch his bread out of the concrete. They felt it afforded opportunities just that great.[7]

Dorsey did not easily rest on the secular side of things. At this time, there was a deep chasm within African American communities that saw the street as the land of the devil and the lost, and the church as the land of the Lord and the saved. What torture it must have been to have the music of both the church and the street resonating from within one's soul! Dorsey was not alone in the struggle; there were others who found it hard to split themselves between church and juke joint. Dorsey's life during the 1920s was one of personal struggle that saw major commercial success with the raunchiest blues, his first gospel song composition, two nervous breakdowns, and work as road pianist and arranger for Ma Rainey's band.

During the thirties, Dorsey came to terms with his search for how to work through personal and cultural tensions of the sacred and secular. Dorsey was always a church musician, and he began to write church songs using the musical ideas that were sometimes more associated with secular music. Dorsey was writing sacred songs at the height of the career of a great influential traveling singing evangelist, Arizona Dranes. Dranes, who was blind and a member of the Church of God in Christ (COGIC), began to record and travel during the twenties. Her "jump" piano style was a blend of ragtime and boogie woogie. Unlike Dorsey, as a member of the COGIC church she worked as a religious musician within a denomination that was more open musically. Beginning often as street ministries, as people joined Pentecostal congregations they were invited to bring their musical gifts with them and were encouraged to praise God in the Holy dance according to the Scriptures.[8]

Some members of the congregations in which Dorsey worked as a church musician had trouble with Dorsey's sacred music. There was wide acceptance of a song like "Precious Lord" written in the gospel hymn style. Dorsey's breakthrough to new musical territory, however – most graphically expressed in a song like "Search Me Lord," a song copyrighted in 1948 – troubled many.

Search Me Lord, Please Search me Lord
Why don't you just turn the light from heaven on my Soul
Find anything that shouldn't be
Take it out and straighten me
I want to live right, I want to be saved
Lord I got to be whole.

The piano accompaniment of this song used all of the blues nuances and riffs of the day, and the phrasing of the text, the performance of the song, and the breaks were straight out of what was known as blues. Some members worried that Dorsey was bringing the devil into the church with these new gospel songs that were just a bit too bluesy.[9]

In 1940, Dorsey published a song that became a processional gospel song, and choirs marched up the aisle of the church singing:

> It's a highway to heaven
> None can walk up there
> But the pure in heart
> It's a highway to heaven
> I am walking up the king's highway.
>
> If you're not walking
> Start while I'm talking
> Walking up the king's highway
> There's joy in knowing
> With him I'm going
> Walking up the king's highway.

This song had a strong cadence for marching, it had the motif of the highway and moving, and it had an open-ended section in call-and-response form that could go on until the spirit said stop:

LEADER	RESPONSE
Oh it's a highway	It's a highway up to heaven
Oh, none	None can walk up there
Oh but	But the pure in heart
It's a highway	It's a highway
I'm walking	Walking up the king's highway
Friends deceive me	Walking up the king's highway . . .

And on and on. Dorsey's songs had the choir-stand rocking, and though some had trouble with this much joy in the name of the Lord, there were thousands who seemed to be waiting for that sound and that swing to express what they were feeling about their life journey.

Dorsey's most famous composition, "Precious Lord," came earlier, in 1932, after the tragic death of his wife and child. By his account, one day while struggling with the grief and pain of his terrible loss, Dorsey found his fingers running over the piano keys, and he began to pray in song:

> Precious Lord, take my hand
> Lead me on, let me stand
> I am tired, I am weak, I am worn
> Through the storm, through the night
> Lead me on to the light,
> Take my hand, Precious Lord, lead me on.[10]

This was the same year that Dorsey organized the first gospel choir at Chicago's Ebenezer Baptist Church. The success of the choir was reflected in the increase in the membership and in Dorsey's own pastor, who had not been receptive to his original compositions, finally telling Dorsey to organize one of those choirs for him.

Thomas Dorsey, like Lucie Eddie Campbell and Charles Albert Tindley, worked within church structures; he also created his own business entities that were entrepreneurial and crossed denominational boundaries. He founded the first Black-owned gospel-music publishing house and organized a choir and chorus convention to propagate the new sacred music.

Roberta Martin, who was to become a protégée of Dorsey and a pioneer in gospel in her own right, did not make the audition as a singer for Dorsey's first choir at Ebenezer Baptist. In an interview with Horace Boyer, she related that as she sat stricken, Mr. Dorsey asked her to play the piano and, as a result, she became the accompanist and with Theodore Frye formed the Ebenezer Junior Choir.[11] Martin's family had migrated to Chicago from Arkansas. Martin was trained in Western conservatory piano and at the time of her audition was becoming strongly pulled by the new music of Dorsey.

From the junior choir would come four boys, Norsaleus McKissick, Willie Webb, Robert Anderson, and James Lawrence, who first became the Martin and Frye Singers. James Lawrence sang with the group for a short period and was replaced by Eugene Smith as the group began to travel. Smith was to become the lead singer and manager of the group.[12] By 1936 they were the Roberta Martin Singers and were a larger ensemble of six, with a second female singer named Bessie Folk. This ensemble would go on to set the sound for gospel music. Not just the collective sound, the individual members in the Roberta Martin Singers created the mode for their parts for the classic gospel chorus. Eugene Smith was the tenor and also the commentator who introduced the selections. Norsaleus McKissick established the classic baritone lead, Deloris Barret Campbell was the model for soprano singers, and Bessie Folk and later Gloria Griffin defined the alto and contralto places in gospel. "God Is Still on the Throne," a composition of Roberta Martin in performance by her group, revealed the superior qualities all gospel choirs strived for:

God is still on the throne
Within your bosom, you have the phone

Where'er you walk, you're not walking alone
Remember God is still on the throne.

When in distress, just call him
If you're oppressed, just call him
When storms assail you, and others have failed you
God is still on the throne.

Whenever men abuse you,
Whenever friends misuse you,
When you're in doubt and you can't find no way out
Remember God is still on the throne.

In the recording of this song, one can hear the classic gospel choral sound. One is first struck by the vocal power and the harmony. The singing is accompanied by piano, organ, and drums. The piano style created by Martin became the style for playing gospel piano during the classic gospel era of the '40s and '50s. The piano organ is the electronic Hammond organ introduced into the Black gospel church by Kenneth Morris, a colleague of Roberta Martin and who with Sally Martin formed Martin and Morris, the largest gospel publishing house.[13]

After the powerful opening chorus, Gloria Griffin sings two verses with the other members of the group bedding it with "oohs." Martin liked a strong harmony choral song, and she liked strong passionate soloists. All singers in the ensemble were soloists as well as dynamic choral singers. Martin insisted that every word of the text be clearly understood, and she pulled the group back in volume during the solo sections.

The Roberta Martin Singers, the Thomas Andrew Dorsey Singers, and singers like Sallie Martin and Mahalia Jackson spread the new music with performances at church conventions and at churches that were open to the new music. Martin used her group as a living score – she was a publisher of her songs, only performed songs published by her company, and sold the music at their concerts.[14]

In Washington DC, the headquarters for gospel during the earliest period was the Bible Way Temple, organized from a street ministry by Reverend Smallwood E. Williams. In 1927, when he arrived in the nation's capital from Columbus, Ohio, Reverend Williams was twenty-one years old. At only eighteen years of age, he had become the youngest ordained preacher of the Church of Our Lord Jesus Christ of the Apostolic Faith, a Pentecostal group. In his autobiography, he wrote about the newly arriving Black people who would form the basis of his congregation:

> The migration which had begun at the close of World War I was flowing like a river from the Deep South. Washington like Detroit and Chicago and New York and Philadelphia and Baltimore, was receiving the Blacks. But none of those cities was overjoyed with having us. Nor was Washington.
>
> Cultural, social, economic, and spiritual ties had been cut off from the migrating Blacks' Southern roots. There was the need to find jobs, schools and churches: In short, to put down new roots in the newly-adopted cities of the North. . . . Blacks had endured segregation and barbaric racism all their lives in the South. When they came North, they wanted a new order, something which would give them a sense of personal identity, human dignity, and decency to replace the old one.[15]

Reverend Williams knew that strong preaching was supported by strong singing, and he found great singers among those who became his regular supporters in his street ministry:

The good singing by the Southern voices which accompanied me in song was indeed thrilling. The people were singing because they were happy, and singing because they were free and enjoying the born-again experience. . . . Among those early witnesses and singers who had migrated from South Carolina farm life to Washington were Brothers George and Lester Jones, and their wives, Gertrude and Blanche; Deacon Arthur Strothers, his wife Cora, and their three children, Geneva, Arthurene, and Dorothy; Deacon George Graham, his mother and family. There also were Brother Emmanuel Davis (who always sang "Send One Angel Down"); Deacon Fred Toland and his wife, Daisy; Sister Leola Tinsley (now Mother Leola Hamilton); and Deacon Evans Bobo, his wife, Ada, and their children. They formed the nucleus of the early membership of the Bible Way Church – a real "street meeting committee." And all good Southern singers, every last one of them.[16]

I was introduced to the ministry of Bishop Williams through his daughter, gospel-music historian, singer, and pianist Pearl Williams-Jones. Williams-Jones became a major consultant in my work at the Smithsonian Institution as we began to do research into gospel music. In 1972, I was a graduate fellow teaching a course in African American traditional music at the Howard University School of Music. Dr. Vada Easter Butcher, Dean of the School of Fine Arts, had created a program that trained music teachers in ethnic music, and this included gospel and earlier African American forms. At one of the project's conferences, for the first time I saw and heard Pearl Williams-Jones perform a short program of spirituals while accompanying herself on the piano. The accompaniments she created for her performance were not from the genre of solo spiritual arrangements with piano begun with the work of Harry T. Burleigh at the beginning of the century. First, Pearl performed the spirituals in a subtle, moving, gospelized style, and the piano provided rich accents well centered in the gospel piano accompaniment influenced by her work and training in Western classical piano. The signature piece of her program was the 1740 Charles Wesley hymn "Jesus Lover of My Soul," sung to the piano accompaniment of Bach's "Jesu Joy of Man's Desiring."

> Jesus, lover of my soul
> Let me to thy bosom fly
> While the nearer waters roll,
> While the tempest still is high;
> Hide me, O my Saviour, hide,
> Till the storm of life is past;
> Safe into the haven guide
> Oh, receive my soul at last.
>
> Other refuge have I none;
> Hangs my helpless soul on thee;
> Leave, ah! Leave me not alone,
> Still support and comfort me!
> All my trust on thee is stayed,
> All my help from thee I bring:

Cover my defenseless head
With the shadow of thy wing.

I was astounded by the beauty of the bringing together of the two works in such a moving, collaborative musical partnership. At the time I was not aware that I was witnessing one of the strong tenets of Williams-Jones's life's work. She was committed to finding ways to affirm and call together the best of the West and Africa in the voice of her people. The brilliant arrangement and performance of her signature work, the Wesley hymn, to the piano rendition of the Bach work, was a true marriage of African American gospel music as worship with one of the great European classical compositions.

When I began to document various aspects of the culture of African Americans for the Smithsonian Institution, there was never any question about who would do the central work of laying the foundation for our research and presentation of gospel music. Williams-Jones was the core of the team of scholars who helped to establish gospel music as a proper area of serious concern for the museum. Her association with the Smithsonian began in 1974 as a member of the advisory committee for the African Diaspora Program of the 1976 Bicentennial Festival of American Folklife. For the next eighteen years, we worked together on all projects I conducted at the Smithsonian in gospel-music research until her death from cancer in 1993.

Pearl Williams-Jones's personal history included a rich and unusual struggle to blend church and education. She was born in Washington DC, and as the eldest child of Bishop and Mother Williams, she was, as we say, also born in the church. Her mother was the church musician at Bible Way and Pearl's first teacher. Coming into a family committed to a life of faith and the importance of education, she was one of those children sent by parents and community to become an authority through study in our nation's schools and universities. She went into the university as a student and performed well. She went into the university and became a provocative teacher. When Bishop and Mother Williams and the Bible Way family sent their daughter to college, she spiritually refused to leave home. It was as if she said to Howard University, where she did her college work, and to Overbrook High School, where she taught for ten years, "Wherever I am, there also shall be the shout and song of my people."

Williams-Jones carried the good news of gospel music within the halls of the academy as worship practice, and she also carried the history and evolution of African American gospel music into the academy on its own terms and in a language scholars could understand. In 1975, she described gospel music in an article in the Journal of Ethnomusicology:

> Gospel singing style is in large measure the essence of gospel. It is a performer's art and a method of delivering lyrics which is as demanding in vocal skills and technique as any feat in Western performance practice. Learning or acquiring the art takes time, practice, and dedication. The performing process is so intuitive as to be almost unteachable. The greatest gospel artists are usually those who were born nearest the source of the tradition.[17]

Here is Williams-Jones speaking the language that identified her as one who has mastered the course of Western education, making a brilliant case for the inclusion of gospel music as a course of study, as the most prolific sacred music genre created in twentieth-century America.

In addition to her sharp, innovative intellectual thinking about gospel song, singing, and performance style, Williams-Jones remained strongly grounded in her religious community. Pearl Williams-Jones knew gospel music because gospel music had been welcomed and nurtured in her father's church. As the daughter of a pioneer who was among the first of those to embrace the new gospel music, she was nurtured and taught by the giants in the field. She knew them all, and when she called them to be documented and recognized with honor and reverence at their national museum of culture, they came.

For me, whose specialty was nineteenth-century congregational styles and folk traditions of the twentieth century, Pearl's presence was invaluable. She introduced me to a range of African American sacred music that had not been a part of my experience. One special memory was the magnificent shout-band tradition of the United House of Prayer for All People, the strongest sacred brass-band tradition we have, with trombones as the lead instrument.

Pearl Williams-Jones was the principal scholar in the Roberta Martin Conference, with three reunion concerts and with a reunion of nine singers: Eugene Smith (leader), Deloris Barret Campbell, Gloria Griffin, Norsaleus McKissick, Romance Watson, Archie Dennie, Bessie Folk, and Louise McCord. The scholars assembled for the panels with Pearl and myself became the core of the research teams formed to conduct primary research in gospel-music history. The teams included Horace Clarence Boyer, the leading scholar in gospel-music performance and compositional analysis, and Portia Maultsby, whose work showed the connecting exchange between secular and sacred genres.

Williams-Jones not only looked to the history of gospel music, she was also a supporter and mentor to the young composers who, during the late 1960s, began to push the boundaries of gospel, expanding the musical language with new dynamic blends of jazz, traditional gospel, the secular forms of rhythm and blues, rock, and Western classical traditions. This new stage of evolution would be called contemporary gospel.

Following in the wake of Edwin Hawkins's 1967 breakthrough recording of "Oh Happy Day," Williams-Jones introduced me to a young gospel composer and leader of a small ensemble called the Celestials, the first gospel ensemble of Howard University students and the first gospel group to perform at Switzerland's Montreux Jazz Festival. The leader of the group, Richard Smallwood, is today one of the most talented and prolific composers working in contemporary gospel today. His work and his performance ensembles are among those that set the standards for this new, expanding genre. His group, The Richard Smallwood Singers, was the first African American gospel group to perform in the Soviet Union. His first album, *The Richard Smallwood Singers*, was on the Billboard gospel chart for eighty-seven weeks.

Richard Smallwood was mentored by Williams-Jones. It was at her father's church, Bible Way, that he had the opportunity to sit at the foot of the gospel piano of Roberta Martin and Lucie Collier Smith. Williams-Jones selected Smallwood as pianist for the Roberta Martin reunion concerts that were a part of the Smithsonian documentation of gospel (Robert Pike played the Hammond organ).

Richard Smallwood grew up in Washington DC and in the church. Born in Atlanta, Georgia, in 1948, he was ten when his evangelist father, Reverend C. L. Smallwood, known as an organizer and builder of churches, settled in Washington. Richard's gift for music became apparent at a very young age. His parents told him that while still in the crib, and before he could talk, he would hum hymns he had heard at church. His father was a pianist, and Richard, as soon as he could climb up to reach the piano, was tapping out melodies by ear. By the age of seven he was playing for church choirs. His mother looked for a teacher for her talented son and at the same time made sure he heard music of all kinds. Richard treasured going to the symphony with her on Saturday and Sunday afternoons.[18]

Smallwood's practice of playing by ear and from memory continued with his first teachers until he entered Howard University Preparatory School of Music at the age of fourteen. His piano and theory teacher, Anne Burwell, took it upon herself to make sure that Smallwood would be musically literate. When he began his college studies at Howard, he found that he was well ahead of many of his peers in musical training because of the dedication of Ms. Burwell.

Richard Smallwood's goal at Howard University was to study music. However, like many other students, he was concerned that this school, organized for the education of African Americans, offered no courses in African American music. Smallwood loved Western classical music, and he also loved gospel and many of the other genres created within African American culture. During this period at Howard you could be penalized if, as a music major, it was discovered that you were performing jazz or gospel music. But this notion was about to be challenged.

In 1968, Howard University, like many other campuses through-out the country, was challenged by radical students taking over and sometimes holding hostage administrations and boards of trustees, if they could get them. At the heart of this struggle by African American students was a challenge to the academy to correct the absence of African American history and culture from the curriculum. There was also a boiling anger at the role of leading scholars who, while guarding the doors to the world of higher learning, had played a major role in the distortion of African American history and contributions in a way that directly aided the oppression of its people. At Howard University, gospel music was not included in the curriculum, and its validity as music worthy of study became one of the issues of the struggle.

In 1969, the Celestials, with Richard Smallwood at the piano, performed in the Andrew Rankin Chapel on Howard's campus in a program for one of the sororities. The Celestials were the first small gospel ensemble on campus organized by Donny Hathaway. Smallwood took over as pianist once Hathaway moved on to develop his professional and very successful popular music career. There was such a negative response from the voice department faculty because of the performance of gospel on the campus that the student performers decided they had to address the issue directly. They decided that the Howard University campus needed an old back-home revival hour.

In developing the choir for the revival hour, Smallwood and the other organizers found that they could only find rehearsal space in Howard's School of Divinity. Howard's School of Music was founded by Dean Warner Lawson, a brilliant musician and choral director. Dean Lawson, known for his work in the preservation of the concert spirituals, was not supportive of musicians who came to Howard to study music and who also wanted to continue their performance of jazz, rhythm and blues, and gospel, musics that they had brought to the campus from their communities. There was a ban in the School of Music on the use of practice rooms for the playing of jazz, gospel, or rhythm and blues.

The clash between the conventional music curriculum, with its primary emphasis on European classical music studies and some attention to the concert spiritual, and the concern of students wanting the full range of African American musics to be included was a long and grievous one. In a protest during the fifties, a group of music majors who were also jazz musicians had staged a noontime concert in front of the Fine Arts building. So there was a history to the energy galvanizing around the old-time revival hour event.

Smallwood relates that at the first rehearsal there were twenty members, but by the time of the revival there was a choir of over two hundred. The response to the revival was overwhelming and powerful. Supporters came from the student body and faculty, so the leaders of the choir – Richard Smallwood, Wesley Boyd, and others – decided to continue its development. They found that they could not use Howard University in the name of the group, so the choir became the Howard Gospel Choir.

The revival hour and the formation of the gospel choir were a continuation of the larger student-led shutdown of the campus in 1968 that resulted in a lockup of the board of trustees. At the heart of this struggle was a challenge to the academy over the absence of African American studies from the curriculum. When the campus reopened after the shutdown, concessions for changing the curriculum had been won, and at the 1970 commencement there were two choirs, the Howard University Concert Chamber

Choir and the Howard Gospel Choir. It was the first gospel choir organized on a college campus.

The musicians who organized the gospel choir also had a deep love for European classical music as well as African American music genres. As students they experienced direct oppression from African American music departments, which were extremely hostile to music that fell outside of the conventional Western, European canon. In some way, these students shared some resonance with gospel pioneers, like Thomas Andrew Dorsey, whose conflicts were between the advocates of traditional genres of church music – anthems and hymns – and the new gospel compositions tinged with the street music of jazz and blues.

When I arrived at Howard in 1971 to begin graduate work in history, I found that there was a gospel choir, but it had no affiliation within the School of Music. So there had been progress, but the world was and still is waiting for full integration of African American musics into all phases of the curricula of music departments.

Pearl Williams-Jones, who had studied music at Howard during the 1950s and had worked out her creative language outside of the practice rooms and classrooms of Howard, was open to changes that seemed to revolutionize gospel music. She was an activist scholar and mentor, recommending Richard Smallwood for his first appearances in Paris and recommending him to me when we began our work at the Smithsonian.

In 1998 I had the opportunity to include Richard Smallwood in his newest configuration, a choir he calls "Vision," when I curated three concerts in gospel music for the Smithsonian at the Cité de la Musique in Paris. Smallwood sets the standard for superior compositions in contemporary gospel. His music creates an interesting dialogue between traditional and classic gospel and the exciting blends that make up contemporary gospel. In his recording *Testimony* (the last recording he made with his smaller ensemble, the Richard Smallwood Singers), he paid tribute to his mentor, Pearl Williams-Jones, with a special arrangement of her composite rendering of "Jesus Lover of My Soul." His 1996 recording on the Verity label, *Adoration: Richard Smallwood, Live In Atlanta*, with his choral ensemble "Vision," opens with a symphonic work, "Prelude," composed and conducted by Mervyn Warren.[19] "Prelude" segues into his majestic anthem "Total Praise," a song poem based on the opening verse of Psalm 121, "I lift up my eyes to the hills; from whence does my help come? My help comes from the Lord, who made heaven and earth":

Lord I will lift up mine eyes head to the hills
Knowing my help is coming from you
Your peace you give me, in time of the storm
You are the source of my strength!
You are the strength of my life!
I lift my hands in total praise to you.

You are the source of my strength!
You are the strength of my life!
I lift my hands in total praise to you.
A- -men- - - - - - - - - - - - A- -men- - - - - - - - - - - - -
          A- - -men A- - - - -men A- - - - -men, A- - - -men
A-men- - - - - - - - - - - - - A-men- - - - - - - - - - - - - - -
          A- - - -men, A- - - - -men A- - - -men, A- - - -men!

On paper, there really isn't a way to take you to the heights that are reached in the coda of this magnificent anthem, based in the gospel-hymn genre. You just have to get to a live performance of this work, fast becoming a required work in the repertoire of contemporary gospel choirs, be they church, community, or school; or barring that, get the CD and join the shouting congregation.

As we near the end of the twentieth century, gospel, the sacred music of the great migration, continues to evolve within and with the African American community, and gospel music has also made major inroads within the music industry, expanding its influence to include national and international popular music spheres. As church music, the gospel community has also grown as other denominations began to form their choirs during the 1970s. This includes denominations initially hostile to the form – Catholics, Presbyterians, Congregationalists, and Episcopalians are among those who have formed their own gospel choirs. Bridging the gap between the commercial commodification of gospel is the formation of community-based gospel choirs in the United States, Europe, Africa, and Australia. There are also mass choirs organized by regions and states, and by national gospel organizations and those founded for specific events. There are collaborative works with gospel musicians working with symphony orchestras in concert halls. There are also gospel operas and gospel musicals. Beginning with Langston Hughes's Black Nativity, introduced on Broadway in 1961, there has been a long and steady stream of gospel musicals. In 1983, Lee Breuer and Bob Telson produced a gospel-based musical version of Sophocles' Oedipus at Colonus, called The Gospel at Colonus.[20] The new innovators, pushing the genre passionately, feel that there is no place where the praise of God and gospel should not be. The range is great and expanding – from the work of Evelyn Curenton Simpson with the Kennedy Center Mass Gospel Choir series, to the groundbreaking work of the late Rev. James Cleveland with the Gospel Workshops of America, to the Bobby Jones Gospel Expo and a nationally syndicated gospel television show, to gospel as a category on the music industry charts, to the film *The Preacher's Wife* (starring Whitney Houston and also featuring the Georgia Mass Choir), to R. Kelly's Grammy–award-winning hit "I Believe I Can Fly," a song written for the film *Space Jam*, becoming a staple in gospel choirs' repertoire – gospel marches on, with no boundaries in sight.

The African American Congregational Song Tradition

Deacon William Reardon Sr., Master Songleader

When African Americans moved from our rural, country, farm-based lives to try on the city, we did not draw a clean line between the rural and the urban.[1] In fact, during the first four or five decades of this century, as we struggled to chisel spaces in cities that were not yet cemented against us, we found that it was not best to be in these strange, cold, new places of our new present and future without some of that precious stuff that had held us steady back home. This is not something you can pack in a suitcase, or ship in a box, or mail in a letter. I am talking about what you carry inside your soul, portable, going with you wherever you go. Only you can stamp it out or deny its existence. More than memories, we move with sounds, ways of being, hungers and itches that need to be scratched just so. Even without a drum there are the rhythms, without a song there is a singing stowed up needing to find the air, and there is knowing ordered by generations that plowed this land and their lives with sorrow and glory. And wherever we go, we can carry this load with us and have it as material to form our new present if we make it so.

It is much of the story of one Deacon William Reardon Sr., considered by his fellow members of the Southern Baptist Church to be one of the strongest hymn leaders of their and many other congregations. By "hymn leading" they meant leading in the lined hymn tradition, that process where the leader chants the text of the hymn and then raises it in a tune that is caught up by the congregation. So if the song was "Guide me oh Thou Great Jehovah, pilgrims through this barren land," the tune in the hymn book would not be heard. Rather, it would be a tune familiar to African Americans, especially in congregations before there were instruments or printed scores to set the melody.

I arrived home from travel on Friday, December 12, 1997, and found a message from Pamela Rogers, a close friend, informing me that Deacon William Reardon Sr. had died at his home on Saturday, December 6, and his wake and funeral service would be the next day at his church. I quickly rearranged my schedule because I needed to be among those who gathered in celebration of his life.

As I got ready for the service, I kept thinking about Deacon Reardon, whom I had met for the first time in 1989. He was important to my work as a historian doing research on African American sacred music worship traditions, and this man with a soft gentle countenance and a strength that ran deep had an expanding, personal impact on my spiritual and musical growth in what now seemed like too short a time.

At the time I met Deacon Reardon, I was director of the Program in Black American Culture at the Smithsonian National Museum of American History. One of my projects was working with Spencer Crew, curator of what was to be a ground-breaking exhibition, "Field to Factory: Afro-American Migration 1915–1940." Spencer asked me as a part of my responsibilities in community outreach and audience development to organize an oral history project, interviewing people in the Washington DC area who had migrated from rural communities during the great migration period.

One of the places I sent one of our field researchers was Southern Baptist Church. This congregation, located in Northwest Washington DC, was known for its retention of some of the older practices from the South, especially South Carolina. At Southern, we were led to Deacon William Reardon, the leader of the Senior Choir and one of the strongest hymn singers. Because of my experience in hymn singing, I conducted the interviews.

Deacon Reardon was what we would call a gifted singer, meaning the path he traveled toward mastering whatever it was he did with such brilliance was not clear to the rest of us, was not the usual process and not in the usual time. When I asked Deacon Reardon where he learned to raise hymns, he said that he didn't:

> Nobody has never told me or taught me how to raise a hymn; this was a gift given to me by God. I can't help but say it was a gift because I remember when God give me the gift. I'm not ashamed to tell nobody because it was given to me and nobody else. And I don't know of nobody in my church even now down there, that was ever able to raise a hymn like me.
>
> Now that's been seventy years ago, but I have never forgotten it. I never will forget it if I live a thousand years. I guess I was six years old and I was by myself going to the pea field to pick peas. I was going up this hill – I was by myself – and I had a little bucket of water, about half a gallon bucket of water. That's all I could carry. And that hymn come to me. This hymn just came to me out of the clear blue sky:

I Heard the Voice of Jesus say
Come unto me and rest

Lay down thy weary one lay down
Thy head upon my breast

. . . and I knew it was common meter. Wasn't a soul around but me, so this was a gift that God give me, to raise a hymn.

I went on back home, I was living with my grandfather, Jasper Reardon, he was a deacon of the church, but he was not a hymn raiser. But my uncle was a hymn raiser and he was the leader of the choir and I was named after him. There was my stepgrandmother, Uncle Willie, Uncle Babe, Uncle Norris, my Aunt Martha, she was in the house at that time and I told all of them that I could raise a hymn and none of them believed it. So I said I can show you. So they said, "Raise it" and I did, just like I did just now for you. Never a one of them have ever taught me how to sing or what a meter was. They were astonished, once I raised it and they sang it with me.

This was before Deacon Reardon had been converted, baptized, and became a member of the church.

I wasn't thinking about joining no church. I didn't join the church until I was about ten or twelve. The next time I was in another church, not my church, there was this minister, he was always trying to help young people. He was in the pulpit and I was in the amen corner. He said, "Who of you young people can raise a hymn?" And first thing, my hand went up and I was the only one that raised my hand. He said, "Well I'm gon give out a hymn and see if you can raise it." And he gave out the hymn:

I was a wandering sheep
I did not love the fold

I did not love my father's voice
I loved far to roam.

I said sure I can raise it, so he said raise it so I did and that church went wild. When I received the gift, all hymns and tunes ran through my mind.

In the first interview, Deacon Reardon told me about the Senior Choir at Southern Baptist, which he led. It was a vocal choir, meaning that they sang with no other instruments except the voice. He told me about the prayer-band meetings and invited me to come. That led to a multiyear association that introduced me to what was for me a new congregational tradition, one that was very old and based in a certain section of the Carolinas. I went to his funeral service with all of these experiences and memories swirling in my heart and soul.

Born in Southwest Georgia, I had grown up in a Baptist church, and for the first eleven years of my life, all of my music was unaccompanied. But the choral tradition was different from the Carolina style and repertoire Deacon Reardon introduced me to. When I joined the church at the age of eleven, so did several other young children near my age. The elders of the church decided that if they were going to keep young people in the church and keep us interested, they needed to have something other than the older traditions in the worship services. They organized a gospel choir, giving me my first experience with singing with an instrument other than my voice.

In spite of that wonderful experience, it's interesting to me that, as a singer, I was stamped with the older tradition. I am an unaccompanied singer; I sing most of the time with other voices and without other instruments. That is the music I heard from the time I was born until I was eleven and then continued to hear around me in devotional services and revival meetings even after the gospel choir was formed.

Deacon Reardon's life as a master songleader and teacher and his passing give me a chance to talk and write about my great passion, African American congregational singing. This is the tradition in which the singing for a gathering comes from those who fill the pews. Songs are raised by a songleader and survive and fill the air and the hearts of those souls who with their voices, hands, and feet give it life. One learns this style in performance by being in church. I was born to my tradition. It was what I heard sitting on my mother's lap. It formed my first definition of what singing was. Everybody who had the willingness and the need sang all the songs with all their strength, and when the spirit was there, there was nothing better. Deacon Reardon talked about the role of the spirit in his singing.

> Above all, let me say this, if you are going to sing or pray, or preach, or just get up to make a talk, you may not say it out so people can hear you, but you should say it to yourself and to God – ask him to take you out of it, let Him do the talking or do the singing. What I'm saying is, ain' no way you can sing or preach or pray – until the spirit comes. You might be up there doing something, but it ain' gon' take no effect. But if you want people to be moved, let the spirit hit you, then let it go to them. Because my Bible tells me that the spirit runs from heart to heart. Strike your heart first, then mine. It'll go from me to you and from you to somebody else – that's just how it goes. I know you've seen it, some people get up and sing for a show, try to show off. But I don't, sometimes I'm

called to do anything, I be just as calm, because I know if you don't do it right, it ain' going anywhere. It's just like pouring water on a duck's back, and you know what happens to that, it runs right on off and I don't like mine doing that. I like to have been some help to somebody when I get up to do something.

According to the obituary in the memorial Homegoing Service, William Reardon Sr. was the sixth of seven children of Jasper James and Maggie Robinson Reardon, born November 10, 1912, in Edgefield, South Carolina. He attended the county schools and was baptized at an early age at the Springfield Baptist Church. He was active in church, enjoying singing in the choir and attending Sunday School. After migrating to Washington and getting established in steady work, Deacon Reardon returned to Edgefield to marry his sweetheart, Eva Gaston, on December 26, 1937. They had one son, William Jr.

During our interview sessions, Deacon Reardon informed me that when he came to Washington during the early 1930s, he carried something that assisted him greatly in getting a steady work situation. He had a letter from a White politician from South Carolina recommending him for a civil service job. And as a result of the letter, he got a job as a laborer in the National Archives.

He spoke of his years at the Archives in a way that illuminated a foundational layer of federal agencies in our nation's capital city that often remain out of sight from the researchers or public who use their services. One of Deacon Reardon's most memorable projects was moving the designated furniture and other effects of Franklin Delano Roosevelt to Hyde Park, New York, after his death. The Roosevelts' Hyde Park home along the Hudson was set up as a memorial site for the president. The National Archives also presented many challenges for a young Black man who entered a system that was segregated and marked with racism. During his first decades, Deacon Reardon experienced daily the separate facilities at his workplace. Black people could not go to the regular bathrooms in the Archives. Black people could not eat with White people in the Archives. They actually had different places to take their breaks from White laborers on the staff. When it came to raises in salaries and raises in positions, there were great inequities in the way Deacon Reardon saw himself moving when compared to his White colleagues who had entered the force at the same time.

The obituary gave a synopsis of his work history. He moved to Washington DC in 1933, at the age of twenty-one. He was employed by the Federal Government beginning in 1934, working at the Navy Yard and the National Archives. He retired from the National Archives in 1968 after thirty-four years of service. From 1958 to 1984 he worked at the Washington Post as a clerk, he retired from that job in 1984 after twenty-six years. While working these jobs, he was a self-employed taxicab driver for thirty-five years, from 1940 to 1975.

Deacon Reardon's work history set him apart. He is a member of that special group of human beings, some within our race, some found in every group that rises. These people, like Deacon Reardon, come into young adulthood with the ability and determination to focus their energy and their lives to move. With discipline and steadfastness and physical, intellectual, moral, and spiritual strength, they renegotiate their and their family's place in the world. Deacon Reardon in his one lifetime astounds us – retiring from two jobs and working as a taxi driver at the same time, never stopping, and considering it a blessing to have a chance to throw himself and others into another time place and level. He wanted, in the words of that William Herbert Brewster gospel song, to "Move on Up a Little Higher." He migrated not just from the rural area to the city; it was not just a geographical move. He did not stop until his migration had placed him on a higher socioeconomic rung.

Why do I come to a discussion about congregational singing talking about the life of a man who migrated to the city during this time? In my work with the historical development of African American culture, I have found it inadequate to only focus on musical expression with our academic systems of analysis and description. The music created by our people seemed to me so connected to the communities that to pull songs and singing out as cultural products seemed to miss an opportunity to know what the songs and singing really were. In trying to understand African American development during this century, I have come to be pulled strongly by what we did culturally as a people as we moved from our old places to new places looking for something better. Our cultural expressions always seemed more than songs and food and hairstyles and clothes and talk. How can you know the political, social, and economic range of a community if you don't know how they signature their identity with their soundings?

This is a twentieth-century story, and when most people think about twentieth-century sacred music, gospel music comes to mind. And rightly so, for gospel is the signature sacred music genre for this century. When you hear gospel, you experience a twentieth-century phenomenon, and the act itself identifies and places you in the twentieth century, within a tradition formed in newly organized – or transformed by the migration – urban African American churches. And the choir is the singing ensemble that brought gospel music into the worship service of these congregations.

Now this does not mean there were no choirs in Black churches before gospel choirs. There were choirs that sang anthems and spirituals, and there were choirs in the South that did shape-note singing. Deacon Reardon's church had such a group:

> When I joined the church in Springfield, it had been orga-
> nized for years and they had a senior choir. When I went with
> them to different churches and heard them sing, I became
> interested in joining the choir. I was the youngest person on
> the choir. There was a junior choir that sang at programs,
> but we had a singing convention once a year. I was a member
> of the senior and junior choir, and we would order books and
> select two songs and rehearse them for the convention. They
> would sing in the convention along with the senior choir.
> The convention was in November and April twice a year. We
> didn't have no piano. There wasn't no piano to be found.

Deacon Reardon is describing rural churches with organized choral units that had rehearsal and songbooks and annual conventions. The books were shape-note songbooks, and that style was the genesis of most choral groups found in rural churches during the early part of the twentieth century. However, in most traditional rural churches during the first four decades of that century, the primary music was congregational and unaccompanied. We sometimes call it a capella: basically you are talking about people who get together and sing, and there are no instruments other than their voices, their hands, and their feet.

When Deacon Reardon came to Washington DC, some part of him understood even as a young man that in order to run for a long time, one had to be constantly nurtured by something. And for Reardon this meant as he moved forward into a new life, he dragged a lot of the old with him as grounding. His church membership, work, and family were central to his foundation as he built a new life for himself in the nation's capital.

When William Reardon moved to Washington, he did not move outside of his family. When he joined Southern Baptist, his uncle was already a member. Southern was his uncle's church, and it was an institution of the migration of Black people moving out of the South into the rural areas into the cities. "When I came to DC, my father had been here. My father came here in '24. He stayed until '30, and then he came back home. My uncles were here; both of them sang on the choir at Edgefield, and when they came here they moved on the choir."

The obituary shared the depth and range of his contribution to his church: "He was a Deacon for 59 years, serving as chairman for 13 years, a Trustee for 25 years, a Senior Usher for over 50 years, Leader of the No 1 and No 2 Senior Choirs, member of the Missionary Society (Peter Circle), Flower Club and the Sunday School. He was President of the United Prayer Band and President of the No. 1 Prayer Band of Washington. A member of the No 1 and No 2 Singing Convention (50 years) serving as MC for 15 years and the city-wide Charity Club."

And singing was bedrock to his spirit. Deacon Reardon was already a mature singer when he arrived in Washington, and he became a major force in the development and leadership of a choir at Southern Baptist. The choir was called a vocal choir, and they sang the oldest songs he knew.

Now when I came here they only had one choir in Southern Baptist. It was a small church. It was organized in '27, I joined in '34. I joined the senior choir, and when I joined the choir [it was] for the purpose of singing the same thing I did in South Carolina. When I was in South Carolina, I sang bass, but here the leader wanted an assistant to him, so he took me off the bass and put me on the lead so I just took up the lead. We sang the same songs that we sang down there. The leader was not from Edgefield, he was from Rock Hill, about one hundred miles apart. It's the same region, in other words we sang the same songs the same way.

The Senior Choir at Southern is an interesting construction because it is reversed. In most cases with congregational singing, everybody who walks in the door becomes a member of the singing congregation. So when a song is raised, everybody is a member of the gathered choir of the day. But here is a new church organized to address the needs of people who are coming to build new lives in a new city. At the same time there is an energy to reach for the new, there is also a sense that there must be continuity. So they have a choir at Southern Baptist whose style and repertoire is of the older songs and singing styles from South Carolina.

The first choir at Southern protected and for many decades insured the continuity of the oldest known repertoire. We should keep in mind that the choir is usually the place where new forms of music enter a worship tradition. During the period Deacon Reardon joined the choir at Southern, Thomas Andrew Dorsey, called the father of gospel music, was organizing the first gospel choir at Ebenezer Baptist Church in Chicago. Ebenezer had an older congregation that was being expanded by new members newly arrived from the South. In this case, the new gospel choir served the newly arrived with a new music form that captured the energy of the new urban experience, and it was called gospel.

Southern was to also have its gospel choirs, its Hammond organ and Leslie speakers:

> Then Sister Fuller organized the Young Adult Choir, it was a musical choir. Then three or four other choirs originated from that. At first, we use to sing every Sunday and then we dropped back to two Sundays and then we dropped back to one Sunday. As the choirs got organized and got where they could sing and render music for the service, we give back to them because we wanted to help the young people have a chance to participate in the service. The last choir was a mass choir, and they sang on Easter and Christmas Sundays even if it was our Sunday because they wanted carols and things – music we didn't have. I know Christmas songs in our way of singing them, but . . .

> *Father I stretch*
> *Stretch my hands to thee*
> *Thee no other help I know*
> *If Thou withdraw thyself from me*
> *Oh whither shall I go?*

> *Oh the birds have nests in the top of the tree*
> *And the foxes have holes in the ground*
> *But the son of man he don't have no where*
> *No where to lay his weary head.*

> *I been tempted and I been tried*
> *I got the Lord He's on my side*

I been to the water, and I been baptized
I got the Lord He's on my side.

Step in the water and the water was cold
It chilled my body but not my soul.

I going down to Jordan on the wheel of time
Ol' Death going shake this old frame of mine.

And this is another one:

What you going to name
name that newborn baby
Oh glory hallelujah
Oh glory hallelujah
Glory be to that newborn king.

Some say one thing and some says another
Oh glory hallelujah,
Oh glory hallelujah
Glory be to that new born king
Some say name him Lily of the Valley . . .
Some say name him the Rose of Sharon . . .
Born in manger, wrapped in swaddling clothes . . .
Some call him one thing, believe I'll call him Jesus.

But we don't sing the usual carols and things, so we step aside and let the mass choir sing on our Sunday.

Deacon Reardon was soon introduced to a union of prayer bands based in Baltimore. The Baltimore band, the mother of the union, was organized in 1936 and some of the founding members migrated to Baltimore from Rock Hill, about one hundred miles from Edgefield County. Deacon Reardon helped to found the Number One Prayer Band of Washington DC.

What is a prayer band? What's the function of a prayer band? A prayer band is a small group of Christians, members of their church, who pull together in a small group to have a more intense, communal, prayer-based life. They believe in gathering together to pray, sometimes they visit the sick and take service to the homes of the sick, and sometimes they meet in their homes.

In the United Southern Prayer Bands, Deacon Reardon found another spiritual and musical home. He believed in the power of prayer, and singing the old songs was his great love. He brought his songs to the prayer band, and he learned songs from the prayer band, including the song that was his signature song when I met him:

I learned "Good Time in Zion" in Baltimore; I didn't like the way they sang it so I changed it a bit:

Good Time in Zion, Zion I believe
Good time in Zion, Zion I believe
Good time in Zion, Zion I believe
Oh the Sabbath hath no end.

Sister Mary didn't have but the one child
He was born in Bethlehem
And every time, time that child would cry
She would rock him in the weary land.

Rock your baby, Mary, Mary I believe
Rock your baby, Mary, I believe
Where Sabbath hath no end.

The members of the United Southern Prayer Bands were people

who had moved from small rural communities in the Carolinas, and they were, in their moving, trying to get away from things in the South that were stopping their progress. Most of these things circled around racism. They had to do with limitations in job opportunities. Being born into communities afforded young people no promise of development beyond what they had, or sometimes, if one was in a very large family, it was difficult to fathom maintaining the level of one's parents.

Many African Americans who worked the land as farmers were sharecroppers or rent farmers. The practice of sharecropping was particularly vicious, because it was almost impossible to get out of debt. Sharecropping is a farming or agricultural system in which people who farm the land don't own the land. The land is owned by someone else. The farmer is theoretically a partner. When you, the farmer, produce the product, 50 percent goes to the person who owns the land and 50 percent goes to you. However, all of the money needed for the seeds and the equipment rentals comes out of your 50 percent. The owner of the land pays nothing for the expenses. Worse, the records for the expenses, and the determination of how much product you made, were kept by the owner of the land, who was usually White. If this person said your debt was $300.00 and you didn't think it was that much, you could not contest a White man's word without putting yourself in great jeopardy.

In the initial years after Jubilee, sharecropping allowed us to set up partnerships and work independently from the landowners. We worked the land and then were paid when the crops were sold. But this system, which at first gave us a little independence, very quickly was twisted to shackle us to unending debt. Also, even though the sharecropper was actually the farmer, the sharecropper was not viewed as a farmer but a worker. Farmers were considered owners of land. So sometimes, when it came to us that things were not going to ever get better, and better was what we had to try for, we moved. And since we were in debt, when we moved, sometimes we had to slip away in the night.

Rent farming was another system that many thought was a little better than sharecropping, because the use of the land belonged to the farmer for the season. The problem with renting the land is that, again, the owner of the land sets the rent fees. In years where prices for cotton were high, rents were raised. If two years later it was a devastating year, the prices fell, and you could not get a decent price for the products you raised, the rent did not go down. So sometimes we left a situation we felt powerless to improve. It just got to the point where some people had to find out whether this United States of America had another place for them to be.

With these stories and a thousand others, with their own uniqueness and their sameness, Black people left, moving into the cities in such numbers that what was known as "urban America" was transformed. With their very lives, they moved to see what else was there for them and for those who would come after them.

Keep in mind that as Black people moved into cities, most of us stayed in the South, on the land, and struggled there. Sometimes in the same rut and sometimes inching or jerking ourselves forward anyway. As hundreds of thousands moved – hundreds and hundreds of thousands stayed, rocking and standing still, moving and waiting and searching, but that is another story. Here we are looking at how some of the people, William and Eva Reardon among them, moved, and in their moving invented ways, while straining to be in motion, to maintain their solid ground.

In Deacon Reardon's funeral service the singing was led by the Singing Convention, in which Deacon Reardon had been a member and teacher for more than fifty years. This Convention sang by the shape-note method.

In one of our sessions, Deacon Reardon gave me a brief lesson in shape-note singing:

Shape-note music got lines and spaces and then its got measure bars. You see from here to here, this is four over four. This is your measure bar and all these notes between the measure bars get four beats total. One, down, left, right that's the way you count it [drawing a design in the air].

Now you see here, this is four over four, but this is a 16th note and this is an 8th note. You see this note that's open with no flag, that's a half note, and if the note has a dot behind it, its gets another half. So this half note gets two beats, but with the dot behind it, it gets three beats. The three beats is for the soprano, and it gives the altos time to run their lines. You have to pay attention to everything.

I learned the keys from the Rudiments, which gives you everything about music. [Then Deacon Reardon sang the soprano or top line on the notes.] That's the music. You got to set it according to what it is. You got seven keys, wherever these notes are setting you got to set it so everybody can set right in.

I can sing all of these, but when I am in the choir, I sing lead, I sing soprano because I am the leader. If we are in choir rehearsal and the bass doesn't know his part, then I go back and help him run his part and help the tenor run his part, and help the altos run their part. And I taught myself, I did not go to class, I just got to studying it and it just come to me.

The service also had a space for a few people to speak who had known and worked with Deacon Reardon. Deacon Willie Allen, Vice President of the United Prayer Band No. 1, spoke about coming to Washington and getting a job at the National Archives and having Deacon Reardon there to show him how to handle himself in that situation. Deacon Reardon took him to his church. He did not ask him to join, but took him there. Deacon Allen decided himself to join Southern. Deacon Reardon took him to the Prayer Band and for him that was it, he was grounded. Deacon Allen sang the first song he heard Deacon Reardon lead in the prayer band:

> You know I been tempted and I been tried
> I got the Lord on my side
> I been to the river and I been baptized
> I got the Lord on my side.
>
> I step in the water and the water was cold
> I got the Lord on my side
> It chilled my body but not my soul
> I got the Lord on my side.

As people talked they shared not only how Deacon Reardon had lived but how one moved from the farm to the city. If you were blessed, someone, family or friend, had moved before and gave you a foothold. If you moved alone, you reached out at work, at church, and found a circle of people who shared like loves and began to build anew.

At Deacon Reardon's invitation, I went into Southern Baptist Church one Saturday, and the United Southern Prayer Band anniversary was in process. By this time, Philadelphia was no longer represented, there were eleven prayer bands from Baltimore, Washington, and Virginia. The size of the bands varied from six to fifteen members. Prayer band members had to be members in good standing of a church, but the bands were not church organizations.

The group of prayer bands in this association had their meetings on Saturday nights, which is a time when churches were usually not used. These were all night prayer-band meetings, and by all night I mean people gathered around 9:00 P.M. with the opening round, singing and praying until midnight. At midnight, they would stop and have a meeting, open the doors of the church, take in new members, take up collections for sick members, and then stop and eat a full meal. They would then come back and start the morning run and go until 5:00 A.M. The first section was led by men, and the morning run was led by women. The first section featured spirituals, hymns, and prayers, the second section featured testimonials and spirituals.

At 5:00 A.M. they would close the meeting and then go home and get ready to go to church. These were mostly elderly people, and I often wondered where their stamina came from. These days the prayer band closes at midnight without the meals. Time has taken its toll on form and frame.

There was a particular style to this singing that I was not familiar with. I asked Deacon Reardon why the songs started so low. When they would start the songs, one person would raise it, I could hardly hear the entrance. But those gathered knew that the air had been stirred and they tended to chime in harmony by the tail end of the first line. They could hear or feel it and they were there with their voices to be sure the song would not falter in its birthing:

Give me Jesus, give me Jesus
That is all I want, give me Jesus.

Room done got dark, give me Jesus . . .
Moving on down the line, give me Jesus.

The better songs you have, if you start them low and let them rise, you will get more essence out of it, and the people get more out of it. It's just like running a race, you don't start out running as fast as you can, you start off easy and then you pick up. If you start too fast you leave the people behind you. It's an intake I have taken in mostly from the prayer band. If you start off nice and soft, then when that music gets into the people, it takes off.

This is South Carolina, but it is not the only choral tradition in South Carolina. This is different from my tradition in southwest Georgia, and it is different from the Sea Island cultures of South Carolina and Georgia. The Senior Lights from Johns Island, South Carolina, sing a song called "Run Mary Run":

Run Mary run, (Whoa) Run Martha run (Whoa)
Run Mary run I say
You got a right to the tree of life.

Little Mary you got a right . . .
You got a right, you got a right . . .
Hebrew children got a right . . .
With all them sorrows, got a right . . .
Weeping Mary, you got a right . . .
Come to tell you, you got a right . . .
Cross is heavy, but you got a right . . .

Ups and down, but you got a right . . .
Children gone, but you got a right . . .
Oh weeping Mary —

The United Southern Prayer Bands also sang a song called "Run Mary Run" with a different tune and text.

Run Mary Run, you know heaven is a shining
Run Mary run, I been running all day long.

Move Mary move, you know heaven is a shining
Move Mary moving, I been moving all day long.

In my father's house
There is a little table
On that little table
There is a little book
In that little book
You know there is a little writing
And none can read that writing
But the Holy sanctified.

So I asked Deacon Reardon why he started his songs so quietly with a beginning so soft and fragile that it comes into life in need of help and you give your voice to the song to help it out. Now I did not say "help the songleader out." The songleader is not the point. The point, and what is alive to be nurtured, is the song. So when the song creeps into the air through a master songleader, it comes in asking for help so that it might not falter or die unfulfilled.

In congregational singing, there is no soloist, there are only songleaders. The difference between a soloist and a songleader is that with a soloist, they have a part by themselves and, if there are other voices, they are in and a part of the background. With a songleader, you can start the song, but you cannot give it life without the participation of other voices. You may have verses, or you may have a call with others responding, but there is no sense that you could stand by yourself. Songleaders get nowhere unless the congregation takes the song over as its own – then the songleader has something to do, a song to lead, a song to move to another level. Songleaders can start the song, but they cannot finish it. In Deacon Reardon's tradition, this way of starting the song softly is very effective in bringing in the congregation. Other congregations do not use this approach. Southwest Georgia, my tradition, uses a strong beginning lead; the Pentecostal tradition uses a lead that's like a vocal explosion – much power. But here you have the magic of a song beginning in a quiet birth.

In the prayer band, the leader of the band would sometimes rally the congregation to help take the song higher. Deacon Hale would start:

> There's a dark cloud arising
> And it looking like rain
> Know the times getting shorter
> From Emmanuel vein.
>
> Know you talking about a shouting.

Well at the point of "rising," other voices would be in. With "looking like rain," there would be stronger voices, and by "Emmanuel vein" there would be some clear foot patting with sounds of enjoyment in between the lines as the singers anticipated the ride they were going to have in this particular performance of this song. If the song was not moving higher with each cycle, Deacon

Hale would say, "You all gon' have to get on in here, I'm gon' get mine, but if you want to get something out of this, you are going to have to put something in it." Deacon Reardon talked about the leadership of the singing within the prayer bands:

I love to hear [Deacon Hale] sing, there are a couple of songs and he really gets into it – "There's a Dark Cloud a Rising" and "Where You Been." And it takes effect on the people. Deacon Hale is the general leader and Deacon Richmond from Baltimore is the second leader. Old man because you know the way, young man because you are strong. In the last couple of years, my wind is not like it used to be. I am strong for my age. When you sing a hymn sometimes there is a space and I use to be able to raise the hymn and reach back and fill up those spaces, but I can't do it so well now.

But this thing, you jump up there for form and fashion and outside show, it just don't take with me, I just can't go with that. I love good singing, I love good preaching, I love – person get up and pray a prayer, now were you there when them boys prayed the other night, now I'll tell you!

This singing tradition is not like going to a concert where you listen and receive from performers on a stage. With congregational singing, you come with the understanding that what you get out is directly related to what you are willing to put in. And if you are sluggish, a good leader will remind you to come into the room not just with your body but with your spirit and your voice. Get to work so that you can be moved by the songs.

Today, music is often performed where you can sit and see what will happen to you when it explodes out of the starting gate. Sometimes it can have a bombarding impact so that you are engaged or enveloped even though you are passive. You are in church, but in the contemporary gospel choir there is often now no place for the congregation to get in. Some arrangements have left the practice of having a section that can go where the spirit leads. The song is arranged from beginning to end in the Western choral tradition. The congregational element has been eliminated. No space for somebody who wants to chime in, but the song is arranged so that it is stimulating and exciting to listen to.

The founders of the prayer band felt that there is a way that the soul is developed through singing the old songs in the old style. If you did not keep yourself in this practice, a part of your capacity as a human being would be underdeveloped. There is a way in which the soul is more deeply fed by this singing than some of the newer styles. There are feelings you get in touch with in the old songs and singing that are not as accessible through newer forms – rock and roll, rhythm and blues, funk, soul, gospel, or rap. And so, sometimes as they tried to work out a way to survive in the new city, one thing they searched for was a way to keep the old songs and singing alive. At this point we are not talking about songs as music. We are also going beyond songs as singing. We are talking about what people believed you needed in order to be a whole human being.

In one of the tributes at the funeral service, one deacon talked about the fact that soon after he met Deacon Reardon they adopted each other as brothers, and not one day passed where they did not talk to each other. There was also a deeply moving story about Deacon Reardon being there to help out with financial needs when one brother was making his start to get a piece of property. The pastor, Rev. Doom, who preached the eulogy, talked about coming to Southern as a young pastor and having support from Deacon Reardon, who allowed him to be a pastor.

I came to the floor and shared how much those of us who had worked on the *Wade in the Water* project owed to the generosity of Deacon Reardon.[2] He was a master songleader. He did not gain his fame from music videos; most people would never know him as a music giant, but he was. A great voice had been stilled. Deacon Reardon was a singer whose voice was raised in the midst of a crowd. He was one among us who knew the songs that had brought us through times when only a song or a moan could wrap itself around us until change came. These songs and this singing he carried in his bones, in his soul, and he shared them in his church, in his prayer band, in his choir. He was one who believed that we still needed what could only be reached through the experience of being in the middle of a singing congregation being bathed in the sounds of the old spirituals and hymns. And when I came asking him to help us write this chapter of history, he did not hesitate. He was always there and always willing to stop what he was doing and talk to me about the songs and the singing and how they helped to create and balance the life he wove with his family, his work and his church.

"I sing not to be heard, not to be seen, but according to the spirit, I sing by the spirit. If the spirit gets in the song, you might hear my voice raised, you might hear my voice changed. If ever you hear my voice change, the spirit done hit me."

Deacon Reardon is survived by his wife and his son, William Jr., of Fort Washington, Maryland; two granddaughters; two great grandsons; two sisters, Anna Stevens of Wilksburg, North Carolina, and Effie T. Weaver of Columbia, South Carolina; a brother-in-law, Earl Gaston of Philadelphia, Pennsylvania; and all of us who walk through our lives empowered by the sounds of the singing he helped us to create.

Spirituals

An African American Communal Voice

Lord! I got a right!
Lord! I got a right!
Lord! I got a right!
I got a right to the tree of life.

This declaration song of freedom belongs to a body of musical literature unparalleled in documenting the voice of African American people struggling to battle the yoke of human bondage we call American slavery. The songs are called spirituals, named so by the people who created them because they came from the spirit – deep within.[1]

The oral transmission that passed these songs from one generation to another was, and is, powerful and pervasive. As I grew up in a rural African American community in Southwest Georgia, the songs were everywhere. I envision that I began to learn them in the womb. When I came to myself, I was hearing my mother and my father and the churches we went to sing songs such as "Glory, Glory Hallelujah, Since I Laid My Burden Down," "Hush, Lil' Baby, Don't You Cry," "Oh Swing Low Chariot! Swing Low!" "Didn't My Lord Deliver Daniel," "I'm Gonna See My Friends Again, Hallelu," "Nobody's Fault But Mine," "Oh Po' Sinner, What You Gon' Do When the Lamp Burn Down," "Witness, for My Lord," "I'm a

Soldier, in the Army of the Lord," "We Are Climbing Jacob's Ladder," "Let Me Ride, Jesus, Let Me Ride," "Time Is Winding Up," and "Come by Here My Lord, Come by Here." Starting school at the age of three going on four, I heard songs my teacher and the older students sang every morning for devotion. Each morning, school began with a ritual led by a student. We opened with a pledge of allegiance to the flag and the country, then we sang, recited the Lord's Prayer, and every child had to have a Bible verse, and then we closed with another song. During these sessions we also sang "Jacob's Ladder" and "Come by Here," but there was another group of songs that came to me through school that were not a part of the repertoire of songs that we sang in church: "Cried and I Cried Until I Found the Lord," "In That Great Getting Up Morning," "Go Down Moses," "Over My Head, I See Trouble in the Air," "I Got Shoes, All of God's Children Got Shoes," "Every Time I Feel the Spirit Moving in My Heart, I Will Pray," "There Is a Balm in Gilead," and "We Shall Walk Through the Valley in Peace." All my life these songs have been with me, in school, in my father's churches in Dougherty, Worth, and Mitchell Counties, Georgia, and in my high school and college choirs. I sang them as a contralto soloist and as an alto in full mixed chorus and glee club full-harmony arrangements. They seemed to be in the very air I breathed.

My early childhood experience coming during and just after the Second World War was in some way resonant with the rec-ollections of world-renowned concert tenor Roland Hayes, the first classically trained concert artist to include spirituals within the body of his concert programs. Before Hayes, spirituals were performed as encores, as if they were not worthy to be in the same category as the other Western art-song literature. Hayes, who was born twenty-four years after slavery, wrote in the introduction to his collection of spirituals: "I have seen them (Afraamerican [sic] religious folk songs) being born in our religious services at the community Mount Zion Baptist Church at 'Little Row' (now Curryville), Gordon County, Georgia. Here I heard great ritual sermons preached and prayers prayed, and I sang the Afraamerican religious folk songs as a child with my parents and the church folk."[2] Hayes was describing a congregation whose elders were survivors of slavery. His contact with the repertoire came some three decades before I was born. However, in the churches I grew up in there was still the same process he experienced. I, too, learned spirituals while they were being sung, and this quote by Hayes reminded me of a day in church when I saw the entire church learn a song that was new for us. It was a regular first Sunday meeting at Mt. Early Baptist, near the end of service, after the sermon and after the doors of the church had been opened (this is the ritual right after the sermon when people are invited to join the church). A man got up singing: "Oh the Lord, oh the Lord, well he sho' been good to me . . ." It was not a song we sang at Mt. Early. There was some foot patting, but people were trying to catch the swing of the song.

"Children the Lord, the Lord, well he sho' been good to me . . ." Then he gestured, asking us to echo him during the first part of the line and join him on the second part and soon the whole church was rocking with the song:

Oh the Lord, oh the Lord,
Well He sho' been good to me
The Lord, the Lord,
Sho' been good to me

The Lord, oh the Lord,
Well He sho' been good to me
Children the Lord been good to me.

He been my mother when I was motherless,
Well he sho been good to me . . .
He been my mother when I was motherless
Well he sho been good to me . . .

He been my water, when I was thirsty . . .
He been my doctor, in my sick room. . . .
He been my friend, when I was friendless . . .

As the song quieted down and came to a close, the members in the congregation were smiling and nodding at each other, saying "Amen" almost like they had just had a surprising and delicious meal.

My work with studying the spirituals began in college, but not as an academic study – it was purely a personal interest. Somehow, one day in the college library catalog, I found James Weldon Johnson and J. Rosamond Johnson's *Book of American Negro Spirituals*. This collection of spirituals had been published in 1925 by Viking Press. There was an introduction to the spirituals that discussed their importance and their richness.

I was deeply moved by this book. I would read the lyrics and touch the pages. Some of the songs I knew, and others I had not sung, but I loved every page. It was as if I had found a piece of myself in a book. I would keep the book out the allotted time and then would feel the need to check it out again. It was a little like walking into your house and putting on a record of a song you just had to hear that day. One day I went to the library to check out what by then I felt was my book of spirituals. It was not there! Someone else had checked out the book! Panicked, I searched for what I would do. I really needed that book! I went down the row of stacks to see if it was misplaced and was saved because there was another collection by the Johnson brothers, published a few years later. This book was a combined volume that had all of the spirituals of the first volume plus a second volume of spirituals (Johnson and Johnson 1940). In 1926, Viking Press had published a second volume of spirituals by the Johnson brothers; then in 1940 the press published *The Books of American Negro Spirituals: Two Volumes in One*. This combined single volume went through additional printings in 1942, 1944, and 1969.[3] To my great relief, I now had two books to choose from! I moved through the next few years rarely without one copy of this precious collection.

I had always loved books. But I had settled for books taking me to other places. After all, there were no wheat fields waving in Albany, Georgia, or porridge or milk maids with blond hair skipping down mountain trails, or snow or sand dunes. However, I had never thought about books being a way to go inside myself. This collection of spirituals functioned that way for me. It was very revealing that I could, through the written page, receive and expand my knowledge about aspects of my culture that had already come to me orally, and that the power of my engagement with the material could survive the transmission to paper.

Once having discovered the Johnson collection (I now own my own hardcover copies of both publications, and I have bought a box of paperback reissues for gifts), over the next decade I would devour everything I could find in print about spirituals. In addition to collections of the songs with music, I read about the singing of these songs by slaves. I was profoundly moved by Frederick

Douglass's description of his personal discovery of the deeper meaning of the songs and the sounds of the singing loaded with the collective burdens of an enslaved people.

Douglass, born in Maryland around 1820, learned to read and write while still a slave. After he escaped from slavery, he became one of the great American leaders of the nineteenth century. He wrote about these songs in the narrative he published about his life as a slave. He felt that these songs documented a kind of communal worldview held by these imprisoned people:

> They told a tale of woe, which was then altogether beyond my feeble comprehension; they were tones, loud, long, and deep; breathing the prayer and complaint of souls boiling over with the bitterest anguish. Every tone was a testimony against slavery, and a prayer to God for deliverance from chains. The hearing of those wild notes always depressed my spirit, and filled me with ineffable sadness. I have frequently found myself in tears while hearing them. The mere recurrence, even now, afflicts my spirit, and while I am writing these lines, my tears are falling. To those songs I trace my first glimmering conceptions of the dehumanizing character of slavery. I can never get rid of that conception. Those songs still follow me, to deepen my hatred of slavery, and quicken my sympathies for my brethren in bonds.[4]

Douglass credits the spirituals with developing within him the idea that the system into which he was born was fundamentally wrong. It is an important point, because often one accepts the condition into which one is born. In a system like slavery, where open critique is dangerous, the spirituals by their sound become a dissenting voice.

I also got to the end of W. E. B. Du Bois's *The Souls of Black Folk* and found his closing essay on the spirituals. In it, he wrote of the songs coming out of the darkness of slavery: "And they that walked in darkness sang songs in the olden days – sorrow songs – for they were weary at heart."[5] He also considered these offerings to be a deep source of American beauty:

> Little of beauty has America given the world save the rude grandeur God himself stamped on her bosom; the human spirit in this new world has expressed itself in vigor and ingenuity rather than in beauty. And so by fateful chance the Negro folk-song – the rhythmic cry of the slave – stands today not simply as the sole American music, but as the most beautiful expression of human experience born this side of the seas. It has been neglected, it has been, and is, half despised, and above all it has been persistently mistaken and misunderstood, it still remains as the singular spiritual heritage of the nation and the greatest gift of the Negro people.[6]

Here it was, in books by Johnson, Douglass, and Du Bois, words in print that met what I held in my heart, that had come to me through the churches and schools I had grown up with – books that knew my whole name. For me, it was so important to find these statements about something that had surrounded me since my birth and find that it was central to the culture and "knowing" of my people – and to find it in books!

The African American oral tradition is full of stories about the use of spirituals like "I Couldn't Hear Nobody Pray," "Wade in the Water," "Steal Away," and "Run Mourner Run" as signal songs of escape in general or, more specifically, with the efforts of those working the Underground Railroad. These stories tell of how the songs and the singing serve the survival of the community. Spirituals were songs created as leverage, as salve, as voice, as a bridge over troubles one could not endure without the flight of song and singing.

Steal away, steal away
Steal away to Jesus
Steal away, steal away home
I ain' got long to stay here.

My Lord, calls me
He calls me by the thunder
The trumpet sounds within-a my soul
I ain' got long to stay here.

Green trees a bending
Poor sinner stands a trembling
The trumpet sounds within-a my soul
I ain' got long to stay here.

My Lord calls me
He calls me by the lightning
The trumpet sounds within-a my soul
I ain' got long to stay here.

I learned "Steal Away" in elementary school. Every May 1st, all of the Dougherty County Black schools gathered for the May Day Fair. There was a singing contest and an oratorical contest, potato sack races, and three-legged races – all great fun. My school, Blue Springs, was one of the smallest schools in the county, but we always got our share of ribbons. My oldest sister Fannie got two blue ribbons (first prize) the year I was in the third grade. I was six at the time. She got a blue ribbon for singing "Steal Away." She also got a blue ribbon for her recitation of Lincoln's Gettysburg Address in the oratorical contest. By the time of the contest, I had learned the song from beginning to end because our school was a one-room affair and our one teacher, Mrs. Mamie Lee Daniels, rehearsed Fannie every day. In the whispers around the song was a story of how it was used as a call to meetings during slavery, when Black people were not supposed to be gathering together outside the presence of White folk.

It was some years later, when I heard Rev. Pearlie Brown sing "Steal Away," that I really felt this story. It was 1965, when I was working with Anne Romaine organizing a tour of Southern Black and White traditional and contemporary folk singers to present concerts throughout the South. The concept was to have a cultural evening of Southern music from both traditions, emphasizing progressive traditions from both cultures.

On the first tour was a blind street singer named Rev. Pearlie Brown. Rev. Brown was raised by his grandmother, who had been sold as a slave from Virginia on the auction block in Americus, Georgia, which was the central slave auction block for the region of Southwest Georgia. Rev. Brown said he had learned "Steal Away" from his grandmother, who told him that it was sung whenever there was to be a meeting among the slaves. He also said that the verse of the song that had the words, "green trees a-bending," referred to bush arbors the slaves created in the woods to have their praise meetings. By bending and tying bushes, they could stimulate the bushes to grow into a kind of a cove that would be a gathering place for people to come to sing and pray and do other things that were not to be shared with the plantation owners. Rev. Brown sang the song slowly, but with all of the emotion that I had heard in church when we sang the lined hymns. It was not a school song – it had weight, body – a drag to it. I traded in all the "Steal Aways" I had ever heard for the one I learned from Rev. Brown.

As I continued to study the literature on the spirituals, I discovered the disturbing intellectual debate over the origin of this genre of song. Some scholars began to assert that the uniqueness and originality of African American songs by earlier observers had been overstated. Some suggested that the idea that with the spirituals we were looking at a distinct new genre of song could be attributed to the observers being swayed by their belief in the right and developmental capacity of Black people as contributing members of the society in which they lived. Among them, George Pullen Jackson of Vanderbilt University, in his 1933 text *White Spirituals in Southern Uplands*, compared the tunes and texts of Black and White songs and concluded that the similarities meant that their origins were White. According to Jackson, these songs were all from camp meeting songs belonging to White sacred music tradition.[7]

At first I pondered over this debate about what was first – were our sacred songs original? Why was it important? Working out our survival in this land resulted in Black people taking on many aspects of the culture in which we found ourselves. It was the cost of survival. But I was raised to understand that it was not a one-way street, that often the foundation of what has been created in this land came from our culture, our knowledge, and our talents. Why was it important to suggest that our spirituals were revisions of White songs and should not be considered original compositions? As I continued to study American culture, I began to understand the relationship between possession, ownership, and status. Whose property is it? Is it original? One way of shoring up the position that one group is superior is to make that group the source of all things of value, all things believed to be constructive.

If there is any question about knowledge being culturally bound, this discussion is an excellent example. Part of the work of fashioning an African American people who were not equal to White Americans in the post-slavery period was carried out by intellectuals. Leading scholars claiming an objective, scientific method of research and analysis studied our work and ways of living and declared us incapable of original creativity. To think them overtly malicious or sloppy researchers would miss the point. It would not make clear the power of operating from a cultural context driven by racism and proclaiming oneself capable of being beyond one's cultural boundaries. For these scholars, the originality of a genre of new sacred songs created by slaves was unthinkable; so they created analytical models that would demonstrate aspects of the spirituals that were shared with White sacred songs. And with some shared texts, and some shared fragments of melody, the spirituals were declared reworked White sacred songs!

There were those who countered this argument. The essay "The Spirituals" in *The Negro Caravan*, published in 1941, charged an oversimplification of analysis:

Few of the disputants know all three of the musics involved: African music (if the music of an entire continent of different peoples can be so simply categorized); Southern White music of the slavery period with which the slave might have come into contact; and the spirituals themselves. . . . That the slave had contact with White religious folk and minstrel music is no less undebatable than that Whites had contact with Negro music. . . .

Lovers of Negro folk songs need not fear either its detractors or the students of origins. Neither European, nor African, but partaking of elements of both, the result is a new kind of music, certainly not mere imitation, but more creative and original than any other American music.[8]

Several studies during the 1970s went back to published observer accounts of the plantation South in the same way historians used planters' diaries to get a more contemporary view on the process of creation with the songs we called spirituals.

Music historian Eileen Southern described the phenomenon within the context of the camp meeting:

They were singing songs of their own composing, which was even worse in the eyes of the officials. The texts of the composed songs were not lyric poems, in the hallowed tradition of Watts, but a stringing together of isolated lines from prayers, the scriptures, and orthodox hymns with the addition of choruses and refrains between the verses. . . . Nevertheless, from such practices emerged a new kind of religious song that became the distinctive badge of the camp meeting movements.[9]

In acknowledging the shared cultural territory within the genre of what she called the camp-meeting spiritual, Southern wrote of the range from whence new sacred songs could arise:

Most of the congregation was illiterate and, at any rate, it would have been difficult to read by the light of the flickering campfires and torches. As a result, the same kind of procedures were developed at camp meetings as had been practiced among Negroes. Song leaders added choruses and refrains to the official hymns. . . . They introduced new songs with repetitive and catchy tunes. Spontaneous songs were composed on the spot. . . . The new songs were called 'spiritual songs' as distinguished from the hymns and psalms.[10]

Dena Epstein, whose work *Sinful Songs and Spirituals* provides a rich resource of data recorded as observers documented Black folk in song and praise and dance, included a report of a journalist during the Civil War, filed from the camp of a Black regiment near Petersburg, Virginia, just before the battle of the "Crater" on July 30, 1864:

Any striking event or piece of news . . . was followed by long silence. They sat about in groups, "studying," as they called it. . . . When the spirit moved, one of their singers would uplift a mighty voice, like a bard of old, in a wild sort of chant. If he did not strike a sympathetic chord in his hearers, if they did not find in his utterance the exponent of their idea, he would sing it again and again, altering sometimes the words or more often the music. If his changes met general acceptance, one voice after another would chime in; a rough harmony of three parts would add itself; other groups would join his, and the song became the song of the command.

The night we learned that we were to lead the charge the news filled them too full for ordinary utterance. . . . They formed circles in their company streets and were sitting on the ground intently and solemnly "studying." At last a heavy voice began to sing, "We-e look li-ke me-en a-a marchin' on, we looks li-ike men-er-war." Over and over again he sang it, making slight changes. The rest watched him intently; no sign of approval or disapproval escaped their lips, or appeared on their faces. All at once, when his refrain had struck the right response in their ears, his group took it up, and shortly half a thousand voices were upraised. The sound was weird . . . when all the voices struck the low E (last note but one), held it, and then rose to A with a portamento as sonorous as it was clumsy.[11]

A song was being born, right out of the conditions of the moment. It also appears by this account that the song did not extemporaneously burst forth, but that these men, understanding the gravity of their orders for the next day, leaned on that part of their culture that provided voice to what they were holding inside. They knew they needed a song. In their culture, songs and singing were central to creating a sense of balance, if there could be any – songs were key to adapting to different and new circumstances. The writer went on to describe the way in which some songs were topical and passing: "Until we fought the battle of the Crater they sang this every night to the exclusion of all other songs. After that defeat they sang it no more."[12]

The Negro Caravan includes another account. The collector records the story of another song and singing that was created to wrap itself around a member of the community who had suffered a brutal whipping: "I'll tell you, it's dis way. My master call me and order me a short peck of corn and a hundred lash. My friends see it, and is sorry for me. When dey come to the praise-meeting dat night, dey sing about it. Some's very good singers and know how, and dey work it in – work it in, you know, till they get it right, and dat's de way."[13] Beatings, a daily occurrence on plantations, could not be challenged by others without the danger of expanding the punishment to the challenger. The community, with a look, or with hands smoothing salve over broken skin, or with a song resonant with support for the one who has been abused, used a song to offer healing support and understanding.

I been buked and I been scorned
Yes, I been buked and I been scorned
I been buked and I been scorned
I been talked about sho' you born
There is trouble all over this world
There is trouble all over this world
Children, there is trouble all over this world
There is trouble all over this world.

Ain' gwine lay my 'ligion down
Ain' gwine lay my 'ligion down
Children, ain gwine lay my 'ligion down
Ain' gwine lay my 'ligion down.

We cherished the ability to create new songs as we experienced different events worthy of lifting in a song. The process by which some songs would live past the first singing to be passed on to the next generation, while others would be sung for a little while and disappear, a document of a brief time, is not available to us. It is clear that some songs moved to the next generation such that a repertoire held sacred came with us as we moved into freedom and on into the twentieth century.

In the next case, one observer, Elias Smith, wrote of his experience of a group of African Americans who gathered to sing. In this account, he included a phrase from a song that served as a link to two other versions of the same song. One of them I still sing:

> I witnessed . . . at Hatteras . . . a party of forty-two men, women and children arrived from South Creek on Pamlico River. After finding themselves really among friends, they joined in singing some of their simple chants and hymns; and when the party were being transferred to the shore, one of the women, with an infant at her breast, broke forth in exclamations of praise and thanksgiving to God, which in its simple pathos reminded me of the song of Miriam celebrating the deliverance of the children of Israel on the banks of the Red Sea. They walked in slow and solemn procession to Fort Clark, chanting as they went "Oh! Ain't I glad to get out de wilderness."[14]

I grew up with a spiritual that went:

Leader: Tell me how did you feel when you
Group: Come out the wilderness,
   Come out the wilderness,
   Come out the wilderness,
Leader: Tell me how did you feel when you
Group: Come out the wilderness, leaning on the Lord
Refrain: I'm a leaning on the Lord,
   I'm a leaning on the Lord,
   Church I'm a leaning on the Lord,
   Who died on Calvary.

The Fisk Jubilee Singers sang this same song with a twist in the text:

Leader: If you want to find Jesus,
Group: Go in the wilderness
         Go in the wilderness
         Go in the wilderness
         If you want to find Jesus,
         Go in the wilderness, leaning on the Lord

It is probable that all of these songs are related, coming from the same root song, "Go in the Wilderness," with shifts being made as the people's status changed in the church from being lost to being saved and from being in bondage to being free from slavery.

The repertoire of slave songs became somewhat stabilized as it moved through the schools created for Black folk. The success of the Fisk Jubilee Singers and the publication of songbooks with text, melody, and some harmony advanced the stability of this new concert genre of songs. In fact, we may be having this discussion in large part because of the Fisk Jubilee Singers. Most of us know the bare outlines of the story: in 1866 General Fisk of the Union Army allowed army barracks to be used for a school sponsored by the American Missionary Association for the education of newly freed Black people.

I am not sure if our minds are equipped to take us back to that time when more than four million of us moved out of slavery into a fragile, poorly defined, and poorly protected freedom. How traumatic it must have been! Some of us knew that we had to have an education, and with a desperation we poured into the schools that sprang up throughout the South even as the Civil War was raging. Fisk, organized as a liberal arts school, was in fiscal trouble as soon as it got started. While there was some funding for schools organized on the industrial model of Hampton and Tuskegee, schools with liberal arts curricula were not successful in attracting funds.

Very soon Fisk was destitute and out of funds. The treasurer, George White, who was indeed White, also taught music and directed the choir. He decided that a tour of concerts might bring in funds for the school. He started off with a group of singers, and the early signs were extremely disappointing. The group was not well received in a press that only saw African Americans as minstrels and seemed to have little in their culture that would allow them to describe their experience. The monies coming in with the first concerts were not sufficient to take care of the singers and the expenses of the tour. When the singers began to add the spirituals to their repertoire, there was an electrifying change. Audiences responded emotionally to what was a new repertoire of concert music. Music that carried the sound of the slave experience! The singers gained support and respect as more and more reviewers began to acknowledge that this was not just another presentation of minstrels. This was a new genre of music presented within a formal concert format. The funds from the singers saved their school and began a movement of concertizing spirituals that was quite spectacular.

Du Bois, who attended Fisk, paid tribute to this group that made it possible for the school to continue. He wrote about Jubilee Hall, the first campus building built using funds raised by the Fisk Jubilee Singers. "To me Jubilee Hall seemed to be made of the songs themselves, and its bricks were red with the blood and dust of toil."[15]

The singers on that first tour were trained in the Western choral tradition. They knew how to harmonize melodies according to conventional Western choral practices because they had been trained by their director, George White. There were those who were not sure that it was all right to present our songs of struggle and survival to people who had never experienced slavery. Spirituals performed by former slaves to new, predominantly White audiences created the first popular music crossovers on several levels. First, the repertoire itself – songs created by African Americans as a part of our cultural survival during slavery – were now blended harmonically according to European formalized choral traditions. Then the songs and the performances crossed from worship and everyday informal practices to the concert stage, thereby finding a new audience among people who were empathetic but had never directly experienced slavery. These new audiences responded to the power of the feelings carried in the text, melodies, and vocal timbres of the singers who knew of what they sang. The honesty and depth of that response to the Fisk Jubilee Singers and the fundraising potential supporting their desperate determination to save and build their school moved this pioneer ensemble and their supporters past their initial reservations. If taking our most sacred songs to the concert stage would assist us in gaining access to an education, we would do it.

The success of the Fisk ensemble created a movement. All schools seemed to organize groups of singers who traveled, performing concerts of spirituals as a part of their fundraising strategy. Then the movement widened and groups seemed to come from everywhere. Some of us put together groups because we could – we knew the songs, they belonged to us, we could sing them in harmony – so we started our own independent jubilee groups. The schools that pioneered this tradition worried about the growing expansion. Was there an improper way of performing the songs? White was disturbed at the news of competing groups who were not as concerned with presenting this repertoire with dignity and reverence.

Concertizing spirituals occurred during the period when mainstream popular culture was being flooded with negative images of African Americans. As the movement of performing spirituals expanded, there were groups of singers dressed like pseudoslaves, with overalls and bandanas, and then there were groups going around singing arranged spirituals in Blackface. And what about that poster of singers shooting craps advertising a concert of spirituals and darkie songs? Was there a way to present the spirituals as art songs to the public and maintain the integrity of their legacy? Who was in charge?

Everyone. Once performing spirituals from the concert stage became a commodity, an open dialogue was played out in practice. Many who were formally presenting the spirituals from educational campuses taught their students the dignity and reverence with which this music was to be presented. Their students in turn became teachers and taught their students this way of performing the spirituals. At the same time, the need to raise funds sometimes opened faculty and students to requests to sing spirituals from potential fundraisers visiting Black campuses. There was both capitulation and resistance. There were some who began to suggest that not only should the spirituals not be performed on request, these songs should no longer be performed at all. It was time for Black Americans to let go of those things that connected us to slavery.

There were others who believed it was our responsibility to continue to transmit to younger generations the treasures of our past. The spirituals were a part of that legacy. It was important to struggle against representations of the spirituals that were offensive, to avoid stereotyping any group of Black people with insensitive requests to "sing one of those old spirituals." The way forward was led by African American musicians who, during the opening decades of the twentieth century, took over the music departments on Black college campuses, and the concert spiritual tradition continued to blossom. Brilliant musicians – like R. Nathaniel Dett, William Dawson, Hall Johnson, Margaret Bond, John Work, Eva Jessye, and Willis Laurence James, all trained in the Western classical tradition – emerged, and through their work as composers, arrangers, and choirmasters expanded the audience through the twentieth century.

First there was Harry T. Burleigh, born Henry Thacker Burleigh in 1866, who was the first to set these spirituals for solo voice and piano accompaniment. He studied at the National Conservatory of Music in New York City and worked with Antonín Dvořák during his residency there in 1892. Burleigh copied scores for Dvořák and sang for him many of the songs he had learned from his grandfather, a former slave. He served as the baritone soloist for St. George Episcopal Church in New York between 1894 until 1946 and beginning in 1923 performed an annual concert of spirituals.

Following Burleigh, the performances of Roland Hayes, Paul Robeson, Marian Anderson, and Leontyne Price established the spirituals as a part of the canon of concert music for soloists. In the private sector, choirs organized by Hall Johnson and Eva Jessye took the spiritual to Broadway and Hollywood films. These groups were followed by many others, notably the Wings Over Jordan Choir, Leonard DePaur ensembles, the Howard Roberts Chorale, and the Harlem Boys Choir. And at the end of the twentieth century, Kathleen Battle and Jessye Norman in their premiere collaboration presented a concert of spirituals at Carnegie Hall (with Marion Anderson in the audience), continuing the work of shepherding this American treasure to a new generation of her children.

The nurturing ground for the concert spiritual tradition was always the schools that were founded to educate African Americans. Roland Carter, composer, choir director, and graduate of the music department at Hampton University, spoke about the tradition of Vespers at Hampton: "At 6 P.M. in the evening on Sundays, we would gather and for an hour we would sing spirituals, one after the other, harmonizing them by ear and without instruction. I am not now talking about the choir, I am talking about the entire student body of Hampton."[16]

Sometime the richness of the tradition was evidenced outside of the campus. One such example occurred in Atlanta, Georgia, on January 15, 1986, for the first federal observance of the Martin Luther King Jr. holiday. I was in Ebenezer Baptist Church, and the program was late in starting. The late Dr. Wendell Whalum, head of music at Morehouse College, was also minister of music at Ebenezer and, understanding the situation, started a spiritual and for forty minutes led the gathered audience in singing spirituals one after the other in unrehearsed harmony arrangements. Although Dr. Whalum's approach was congregational in that there had been no rehearsal for this spontaneous songfest, the Black members in the congregation were predominantly from Black high schools and colleges and were familiar with the concert spiritual tradition. To this day with a Black audience over forty, I can start to sing spirituals, sing twenty or thirty, and find that those gathered can sing them along with me. How is this possible?

It is the result of the African American educational culture created to provide education for us, and the coming into that system of African American musicians trained in the Western musical tradition who also had a respect and reverence for the sacred songs created by slaves in this country.

Hampton Institute, now Hampton University, had followed Fisk in forming singing ensembles to travel and raise money for the school. The first African American head of music at Hampton was R. Nathaniel Dett, conservatory trained, who came to Hampton in 1913. In addition to his arrangements of spirituals, Dett also created new motets based on the spirituals. Two of his compositions have become a part of the canon of Black choral literature. If your ensemble could sing Dett's "I'll Never Turn Back, No More" and "Listen to the Lambs," and get a superior ranking, this would place you with the elite among Black high school choral groups.

I knew of Dett's compositions, but not because of my freshman college music appreciation class, which was concerned with exposing me to the music of Mozart, Brahms, Beethoven, Handel, and Debussy. I came to college already knowing the music of Dett and Dawson and James, because whenever Ann Elizabeth Wright, my high school chorus director, announced the song we were going to perform, she always acknowledged the composer. I can still hear her saying, "We are now going to perform 'Listen to the Lambs' by R. Nathaniel Dett."

During the summer of 1979, I returned to my twentieth high school class reunion and during the Sunday morning service sang the spiritual "Stan' Still Jordan." Miss Wright had taught me that song as contralto soloist for the Monroe High School Chorus. After the service, Miss Wright came up and asked me if she had taught me that song. I said yes, she had. I was a bit taken aback because she had to ask. I thought she would remember me and the song! In addition to being my chorus director, Miss Wright had been my homeroom teacher for four years and had taught me Latin and French. After all, where else would I have learned it?

Miss Wright by then had retired. During her more than thirty-five-year career at Monroe High School, she had mixed chorus, boys glee club, girls glee club, sextets, and quartets and soprano, baritone, tenor, and contralto soloists – every year. There were thousands of us whose voices had passed through her hands. And she had a different homeroom class every four years. So maybe neither the song nor I was at the top of her consciousness.

Ann Elizabeth Wright was my entrance to the world of classical music from the European classical tradition. She was one of thousands of Black teachers who moved in the twentieth century with the work of shaping new generations of young people for our work of moving the race forward. Teachers were responsible for the uplift of the race. Children must go to school, more and more must go to high school, more and more must finish high school, and more and more must get to college. It was unending, all-encompassing work, and I am marked by the experience and the gift of teaching creating the bridge over which we passed to the rest of our lives.

Miss Wright's colleague, Mr. Arthur C. Searles, who also taught at Monroe High School, described Miss Wright's importance as a presence in that education community: "In her teaching Miss Wright developed the best choruses in the world. Each year her choruses would go to the state choral convention in Macon and come back with the highest ranking of superior. She was a shy person and didn't take the stage easily to display her talents. Her whole heart, mind, and body were wrapped up in music through her students."[17]

I met Miss Wright in 1956 when I entered high school. During those days, when you came into the freshman class you were assigned a homeroom teacher, and her job was to get you through high school. Each morning we reported to homeroom for attendance, devotion, and announcements and returned for a homeroom period at the end of each day. And after lunch, when others had recess, Miss Wright held rehearsals for the choir.

I knew I was going to try out for the choir before I arrived at Monroe. My oldest sister Fannie was in the choir, so I knew that if I could get in the choir, I would be allowed to wear stockings. I was twelve in the ninth grade and a bit young for high school, and my mother was not interested in my wearing stockings, heels, makeup, or "taking company." I auditioned right away, and when Miss Wright started to sing and play "Steal Away," I slipped naturally to the alto line and held it and was in! I got my first pair of stockings, but not a pair of real heels or daily makeup until my sophomore year, but it was a beginning! The Monroe High Chorus repertoire and performances were standard for Black choruses of the period. In the fall we focused on the Christmas Carol concert. In the spring we rehearsed for the spring concert, for the annual state chorus competitions, and for graduation. We learned the "Hallelujah Chorus" from *The Messiah* my freshman year, and it always ended Miss Wright's Christmas concert.

The Christmases of my teenage years were shaped not by commercials and ads that started after the Thanksgiving parade. I moved toward Christmas from the fall with the songs we were learning in chorus rehearsals. In elementary school we had sung the carols "Oh Come All Ye Faithful, "Oh Little Town of

Bethlehem," "The First Noel," "Away in a Manger," but not in harmony and not with a professional choral sheen. Now I moved toward Christmas on the alto lines of the carols, and it moved me to a new place. One of the beautiful new songs I learned was a lullaby:

Joseph dearest, Joseph mild
Help me rock my little child
God will give you your reward,
In heaven above – the Son of Virgin Mary.

When we sang we had to consciously make our voices smooth and controlled – our singing was to be sincere, but unlike the church I grew up in, this singing was not supposed to be a door to having the spirit take you higher. There was no spirit possession in this chorus. We were singing by Miss Wright's direction, and she was guided by the sheet music and years of training. It was different; I was clearly going to places I could not experience if I had stayed at home and been trained by my parents and our church. It wasn't clear then, but in hindsight I see that my parents, even when they did not totally trust people with education to know what was best for their children, knew that there was a bridge that was high school and college leading to a road they wanted all of their eight children to travel.

Among the Christmas repertoire there was a group of songs that were more moving and more beautiful for me, and they were the spirituals. And even though they were spirituals, they were also sung with the smooth voice. You could actually let in a little feeling, but you had to keep it banked so it would not break through and "fire" the song – the opposite goal of singing in our church. Curtis Hayes, the tenor soloist, sang "Oh Poor Little

Jesus"; the male glee club sang "Jesus the Light of the World"; and the mixed chorus sang "Rise Up Shepherd and Follow," "Behold That Star," and "Go Tell It on the Mountain." These were songs the slaves had made to celebrate the birth of a baby born with nowhere to lay his head. How clearly must the slave parents, especially the mothers, have understood Mary and Joseph. How they as slave parents must have longed for an Egypt to flee to when the auction block loomed. The songs touched my heart, and over the years I have added many more to this list begun by Miss Wright.

It was the work after Christmas that made life grand. Right along with Haydn's "The Heavens Are Telling," Miss Wright taught us Hall Johnson's "Ain't Got Time to Die." Jamesina Trent, soprano, did the solo lead. The song, as explained by Miss Wright, was an original composition in the spiritual style by Johnson. It was a bit more churchy with a little more bounce than some of the other spirituals. Trent also performed Florence Price's solo arrangement of "My Soul's Been Anchored in the Lord"; I can still hear her hitting that high note on the end with ease and feel her voice ringing all around us – it was marvelous!

Then there were the arrangements of William Dawson, who developed the famous chorus at Tuskegee Institute. We sang "Ezekiel Saw de Wheel," "Good News Chariot's Coming," "I've Been Buked and I Been Scorned," and "Soon Ah Will Be Done Wid de Trouble of the World." I loved the bass line Dawson put under that piece.

One of the things that would happen at the end of these arrangements was that there was often a big sustaining ending that would leave the sound ringing in the room and through your body after you had stopped singing. This kind of big ending was not a part of my church singing style, in which we generally ended our songs soft and winding down, sometimes moaning the last cycle. The Western choral tradition loved the big ending, and this new ending was integrated into all sorts of music we created during the twentieth century, including many of the arrangements for the spirituals.

Miss Wright introduced me to the work of John Work from Fisk. There were two Works who helped to shape music at Fisk. The first, John Wesley Work Jr., had graduated from Fisk in 1895 and was on the faculty. In October 1898, he sang in a mixed quartet trained by Ella Shepherd Moore for the American Missionary Association Meeting in Concord, New Hampshire. Shepherd had been the first accompanist for the first tour of the Fisk Jubilee Singers. Work went on to organize several quartets and singing ensembles. As lead tenor, he was responsible for the musical direction of the recordings of Fisk Quartets on Victor Records in 1910, Edison cylinder recordings in 1923, and Columbia records beginning in 1914.[18] When Work left Fisk in 1923, James Myers and his wife, Henrietta Crawford Myers, a contralto, took over as manager and director of the Fisk groups until 1947.[19]

During the 1950s, John Work III became director of music at Fisk and added a number of his arrangements of spirituals to the repertoire. Work also attended some of the revival tent meetings that were being held in cities during the 1940s and warned that the music used in these services called gospel was new and that it was going to make a big impact on sacred music in this century. Little did he know at the time that there would be a gospel choir organized at Fisk during the 1970s that challenged the primacy of the Fisk Jubilee Singers. When they were not received warmly by some faculty members and school administration, they removed themselves from the campus until they were invited back as a campus ensemble. The song we loved most by Work was his arrangement of "Rockin' Jerusalem":

> Oh Mary,
>> Oh Martha
> Oh Mary ring dem bells
> Oh Mary,
>> Oh Martha
> Oh Mary ring dem bells
> I hear archangels rockin' Jerusalem
>> Jerusalem, Jerusalem, Jerusalem
> I hear arch angels ringin' dem bells . . .
>> Jerusalem, Jerusalem, Jerusalem . . .
> New Jerusalem – –
>> Rockin' Jerusalem
> New Jerusalem
>> Ringing them bells.
>
> Church gettin' higher
>> Rockin' Jerusalem
> Church gettin' higher
>> Ringing dem bells.

During the Civil Rights Movement, "Rockin' Jerusalem" became a freedom song. "Oh Mary, Oh Martha" became "Oh Pritchett, Oh Kelly" for Laurie Pritchett, the chief of police, and Asa Kelly, the mayor of Albany, Georgia. And "Jerusalem" repeated under the solo lead became "freedom." "Church getting higher," became "bail's gets higher" and "rockin' Jerusalem" became "prayin' in jail."

And who was Ann Wright – the woman who opened me to this expanded world of songs? She never married, she lived with her parents and cared for them as they got older. We had a sense that the school and the music were her family. Jessie Johnson, who was a tenor in her choruses from 1965 to 1968, said of her: "I didn't understand Miss Wright and the music that she taught us at the time. She seemed to be from another time, she carried herself in a certain way such that she had no disciplinary problems from her students. In the chorus, she had a wide range of students, from well behaved to thuggish. She could control behavior with a glance or a 'you must apologize.' "[20] Ann Elizabeth Wright was born November 4, 1916, in Macon, Georgia, one of two daughters of Mrs. Minnie and Dr. Noah B. Wright. She moved to Albany, Georgia, when her father was called to pastor the Mt. Zion Baptist Church in 1926. She graduated at the top of her class from Madison High School and entered Spelman College at the age of fifteen, graduating from Spelman in 1936. She received an undergraduate degree from Spelman and a masters from Atlanta University. She taught for thirty-nine years as a choral director and foreign language teacher, first at Madison and then at Monroe High School, retiring in 1975. She believed in the transformative discipline of learning and performing music, believing that "this world would be a better world if people would appreciate music of the highest caliber more."[21]

Miss Wright was part of the infrastructure of twentieth-century African America. Her work was that of transforming the young people who came to her into adults who would not only survive twentieth-century America but thrive in it. When we entered her classroom, we entered another cultural zone. We did not speak

English the way she did, nor Latin, nor French, and the songs and style of singing were new. And yet Johnson recounts:

> She made us proud of ourselves and proud of the music we had to sing. The majority of the music was spirituals and worksongs. My favorite song she taught was "Po' Ol Lazarus," which the men's glee club sang. She taught these songs with the same discipline as any other classical song. These are the songs that brought the most joy to Miss Wright, and these are the songs that brought most joy to us. She demanded perfection and she manifested perfection. She did not for one minute allow us to think that there was something we could not do, or that there was something that was too difficult to do. That gave you a kind of confidence within yourself and the way you felt about yourself. Much of this she radiated not so much by what she said but by what she did. I was a person who was not prone to joining in extracurricular activities. But for some reason, I loved singing in Miss Wright's choir. Even though I was asked to go out for the football team, it was the choir that really held my interest. I ask myself why, and it had to be the way Miss Wright made things always fun with perfection. She was able to combine strict discipline, a drive for perfection with a jovial air. I think she brought that ability from another time and place, from the spirit of those who had known slavery and had known hardships.[22]

McCree Harris, the other French teacher at Monroe, often went with Miss Wright as chaperone on the chorus trips that brought all the choruses in the state together for competition and rankings:

> She played spirituals, classics (European), I never heard her

play popular music. One of the last times I went as chaperone with her, the judges had given each chorus the Hallelujah Chorus to perform. You should have heard Miss Wright play that piano that day! It was like you were in heaven and the angels were looking over the balcony. She had it to perfection. We were in Macon that year and everybody in the place stood and applauded. She played that piano so, she really made it sound like an organ! That was her last music festival.[23]

Ann Elizabeth Wright died January 17, 1988, after a long illness. The concert spiritual tradition soared in her hands, and her students joined others who were so blessed to have learned and grown under the tutelage of one like her. I came to her with spirituals from an oral tradition. I left with more spirituals and an appreciation for the decision and drive our parents and their parents before them had made that we as Black people would go to school, with the hope that those schools, structured to be in service to another culture, would not take us from the source of our strength and survival. Every time I sing the spirituals I learned through her, I think of the tradition that made these songs and the singing of them a part of my ability to stand in this world.

Spirituals record the struggle of a people to survive, but like no other history, they have the power to touch the souls and stir the emotions of the people who sing and hear them. This African American song, with its evolution within American society – like a great river shooting off hundreds of tributaries to be joined together somewhere further down the way – gives us the richest opportunity to view the African American song tradition in a way that unleashes the powerful human story it holds.

Freedom Songs

My African American Singing and Fighting Mothers

I have had singing in my life since I was a young child. However, my experience with the performance of music from a formal concert stage came by way of the Civil Rights Movement and a group called the SNCC Freedom Singers. We were a group of a capella singers, but we were first field secretaries for the Student Nonviolent Coordinating Committee (SNCC), the organization of the Movement formed by student leaders who left their campuses to work full-time against racial injustice in the United States. The Freedom Singers, formed by Cordell Hull Reagon with myself, Rutha Mae Harris, and Charles Neblett (and joined at various times by Charles's younger brother, Carver "Chico" Neblett, and Bertha Gober) began to travel throughout the country singing freedom songs to anybody who would listen. Being a fighter for freedom in the Movement meant that our stages were wherever we were, and the songs were a way of coming together, holding each other and proclaiming our determination as citizens to fight racism in this land of our birth. The Freedom Singers sang in concert halls, schools, living rooms, clubs, folk festivals, in elementary, junior, and senior high schools, in colleges and universities. As a group, our concerts were often a way of introducing and connecting people who wanted to find ways to be a part of the Movement, to the culture and energy of activism taking place in many Southern communities.

As a professional musician, I feel blessed by this premier experience because it formed the foundation of how I began to understand my work as a singing fighter for justice. My music has also been undergirded and expanded by my work as an academy-trained historian – researching, teaching, and sharing the story of the historical development of African American culture. Much of what I do as a scholar and artist is inventive. However, I have always searched for and found models that have helped me to formulate ways to approach different aspects of my work. There were always models – contemporaries and those who came before me, whose life work made me believe that there was a way to be a singer in this world and have that singing at the center of my beliefs and central to my responsibility as a member of the communities in which I work and live.

I began to study history in the late 1960s, during the wake of the most intense period of the Movement. Somehow out of our struggle for full rights as citizens and human beings came a questioning of what we thought of ourselves. Charged by the thinking and teaching of Malcolm X, we moved into a period of reformation and reclamation as a people. Black Consciousness, Black Power, and Black Nationhood were just a few of the names. It was a struggle that was also a celebration. Black people raised in a collective shout – fisted hands! liberated hair! – and challenged and often frightened those who oversaw the maintenance of the authority of the dominant culture. Where was all of this expanding, electrifying cultural energy going to fit? And we didn't fit, we in a collective embrace of ourselves widened the national consciousness about our presence as an American and an African people – citizens of this nation. It was a wonderful time of personal discovery and growth. I can still remember lectures by historian John Henrik Clarke, anthropologist Council Taylor, and historian C. L. R. James that influenced my thinking on the role of the intellectual in the transformation of any society that needed turning over. These scholars provided information we did not have about Africa, and new ways of thinking about the history of our country. It was a perspective we were starving for as we struggled to form a way of being in this country grounded in an appreciation of our worth as a people.

The late 1960s was a time when we created supportive environments in formal and informal community spaces to reconsider the stories that we had been told that demeaned us as a people. I was introduced to the works and writings of Paul Robeson and W. E. B. Du Bois, people who gave their lives to struggle for justice in this world. I had known of Paul Robeson as a singer and had remembered the NAACP's disassociation from his views in the early 1950s, but I had not yet read about Robeson's introduction to African culture during the 1930s when he lived, worked, and studied in England:

> As a first step I went to the London School of Oriental Languages and, quite haphazardly, began by studying the East Coast languages, Swahili, and the Bantu group which forms a kind of Lingua Franca of the East Coast of Africa. I found in these languages a pure Negro foundation, dating from an ancient culture, but intermingled with many Arabic and Hamitic impurities. From them I passed on to the West Coast Negro languages and immediately found a kinship of rhythm and intonation with the Negro-English dialect

which I had heard spoken around me as a child. It was to me like a home-coming, and I felt that I had penetrated to the core of African culture when I began to study the legendary traditions, folksong and folklore of the West African Negro.[1]

During the 1930s Paul Robeson began to write about the richness of African culture: he studied the cultures, went to school with some of the future leaders of postcolonial African nations, and thought it was quite a wonderful thing to be Black. He also knew that African Americans did not get the same information he was absorbing and that we suffered from the deficit.

In addition to being deeply moved and inspired by the intellectual brilliance of Du Bois, I was particularly struck and challenged by his sense of himself. Here was a Black man who thought that if he thought something, it should be published and everybody should read it! I wondered, how did he get that way? Where do you get a sense from your inner core that your existence is part of the answer to the challenges of the time? In an article entitled "The Propaganda of History," Du Bois wrote: "The most magnificent drama in the last thousand years of human history is the transportation of ten million human beings out of the dark beauty of their mother continent into the new-found Eldorado of the West. They descended into Hell; and in the third century they arose from the dead, in the finest effort to achieve democracy for the working millions which this world has ever seen."[2] Here, he was writing about us, Black people, as we were removed from Africa into and through slavery, and then to emancipation and a heroic struggle to make freedom mean more than a new kind of slavery.

As a young woman, my earliest sense of who I could be was formed by my mother, my teachers, and other women in our community. With my involvement in the Movement, I met and was also inspired by the intelligence, power, and courage of women like Ella Jo Baker, who I call my political mother; there was also Fannie Lou Hamer, Septima Clark, Joyce and Dorie Ladner, and Rubye Doris Robinson, who were all part of my activist family.

As a singing participant in the Movement, I began to notice how well the old songs we knew fit our current situation. Many of the freedom songs we sang we had learned as spirituals, sacred songs created by slaves. Our struggle against racism often found us reaching for connections with those who had during the nineteenth century fought to end slavery in this country. Somewhere between singing the songs of our people as we struggled in daily confrontations against racism and absorbing everything I could get my hands on about Africa and our history, I began, in a healing way, to be reconnected to the nineteenth century, beyond the known lines of my biological family. Many of the connections I already knew from stories I had heard in between the singing of the spirituals. However, much of what I share here would have been impossible to know without the practice of history.

It is very heavy work to embrace your links with your past, but sometimes when you do you find riches and new ways to think about who you are and who you can be. I was blessed during this same time to meet and for almost two decades move in circles with an extraordinary woman who had an encyclopedic knowledge of the song culture in which she was raised and of which she was a major carrier. Bessie Jones of the Georgia Sea Island Singers became for me a living link to the culture of slavery, and with great generosity she shared with all who would listen. It was also important to find that the two women I was most familiar with from the nineteenth century – Sojourner Truth and Harriet Tubman, whose names and stories were passed to me as a child – used music in their life-work. The stories I heard as a child presented these women as fighters for freedom for Black people. This chapter is about and in tribute to these three women – Bessie Jones, Sojourner Truth, and Harriet Tubman – whose lives as independent African American women, interlaced with songs and singing, remain a beacon for me and others who understand music as nurturing, energy, and power for making a difference in the world in which you find yourself.

In some way, I feel myself to be a twentieth-century daughter of these three women. They are important to my work as a performing artist because of what their lives taught me about singing and struggle. I understood early in my performance work that even though I loved to sing, I did not come to the stage for the performance of songs. I came to the stage to sing about and for things I care about as a person living in the world.

In this essay, I draw attention to certain experiences in their lives that has greatly influenced my development as an African American singer and fighter. In some cases, I share some of my own story, not in any way to suggest equity of experience, but to illuminate the ways in which their lives and struggle threw light upon my pathway.

I did not learn about Bessie Jones from stories. I actually met and worked with her during the time I was singing as a member of the Freedom Singers. She was a child of the twentieth century, and her teaching would represent a more direct path between those of us who came to adulthood during the Civil Rights Movement and those who struggled against slavery and for freedom in this land.

Bessie Jones was born in Smithville, Georgia, on February 8, 1902.[3] She grew up in Southwest Georgia, the same area where I was born. I was born in Dougherty County; she spent her early years about twenty miles away in Terrell County. I was not to meet her until many years later when she was a singer with the Georgia Sea Island Singers. By that time, she had long been a resident of St. Simon Island, off the coast of Brunswick, Georgia, where she moved after her marriage. The man she called her grandfather, Jed Sampson, was shipped from Virginia and sold on the block in Americus, Georgia. Bessie Jones said that he was a full-blooded African who wore his hair down his back. Jed Sampson took Bessie as a child into the woods and taught her about the herbs that were for healing. One of his lessons was that any plant or tree that stayed green throughout the winter was good for the healing of the body. Jed Sampson taught her games and songs, such as:

Reglar, reglar rolling under,
Gimme the gourd to drink water
Reglar, reglar rolling under,
Gimme the gourd to drink water.

I don't want no gopher snow water,
Gimme the gourd to drink water
I don't want no gopher snow water,
Gimme the gourd to drink water.

Never seen the likes since I been born,
Gimme the gourd to drink water
Bull cow kicking on the milk cow's horn,
Gimme the gourd to drink water.

What is the song about? Bessie Jones always told stories about a song before and after she sang it. In this case, she told us that during slavery, White people on the plantation drank out of glass dippers, and they forbade their slaves to drink out of those dippers. The slaves made dippers out of gourds and the water in the gourd dipper was cooler than the water in the glass dipper.[4] "Gopher snow water" is another way of saying White people's water.

"Reglar reglar rolling under" is a response to a greeting inquiring how you are doing. Someone would come in the house and you'd asked them how they were doing, and they would say, "Ah – reglar rolling under," meaning that this life, this world, these conditions got me rolling under, or I am being rolled under by the wheel of life. And in this phrase you get the feeling of trouble or challenge of one's daily life just turning you under, and in that turning, in spite of it all, you are still moving.

The bull cow, the male of the herd, is also the largest and most powerful. Bulls occasionally fight bulls, but never the milk (female) cow. Slavery was full of examples of those in charge – the planter, overseer, or driver – doing violence to and brutalizing someone weaker or more vulnerable. Often when our behavior is improper, we say that we're acting like animals, but this song makes it clear that the problem is not with the nonhuman animals. Bulls compete and fight other bulls – not the milk cows. However, with humans, in a system like slavery, the powerful dominate those who are most vulnerable: wives, children, slaves, workers. The text of this song chides the planter or any manager who would brutalize the very workers whose labor creates their wealth and status. "Never seen the likes since I been born, bull cow kicking on the milk cow's horn."

I met Bessie Jones for the first time at the Newport Folk Festival in 1963 while I was performing with the SNCC Freedom Singers. Also performing that year were Bob Dylan, Peter Paul and Mary, Joan Baez, Pete Seeger, the Georgia Sea Island Singers, and a group of Black men who had done time in the Texas state penitentiary doing prison work songs. The Georgia Sea Island Singers – John and Peter Davis, Emma Ramsey, Mabel Hillary, and Bessie Jones – were presented by folklorist Alan Lomax, who introduced each song and talked about the songs that were descended from slavery and were still a part of the traditions on the islands off the coast of Georgia and South Carolina. When the Georgia Sea Island Singers walked off the stage, every member of the Freedom Singers met them as they came down the steps. We surrounded them, telling them how great they were and that we wanted to know more about the songs. Bessie Jones said that she would love to teach the songs and the stories.

Over the next decade, I had a number of opportunities to perform on the same stage with the Georgia Sea Island Singers, with Bessie Jones and John Davis sharing in providing invaluable commentary about the songs. It was also during this period that I got my first experience with organizing cultural events working with Guy Carawan, musical director at Highlander Folk School (now the Highlander Research and Education Center). Guy was a musician and activist in the Movement who documented a lot of the music of the Movement and traditional music on Johns Island, one of the islands off the coast of Charleston, South Carolina. At the first conference we did together, the Georgia Sea Island Singers and Dock Reese (from Texas) came together in sessions with movement songleaders from communities across the South. We heard and learned some very old songs for the first time, and we heard stories about some of the songs we had grown up with.

One of the songs Bessie Jones taught us was "Juba." This was a hand and thigh rhythm-play with several stories. First, with the hand rhythms, we were creating drum rhythms. Even though drumming among the slaves was banned in some areas, it was not eliminated. We needed this way of resonating with all of the pulses of our lives and the universe, and we found so many ways to keep drumming. With Juba we drummed, with our bodies being the drums. The words of this "play" protested the unfair and unequal treatment our people experienced during slavery.

> Juba! Juba! Juba this and Juba that
> Juba killed the yellow cat!
> Bent over double-trouble Juba!

Recently, in demonstrating this song and rhythm to a friend from the West African nation of Guinea, I was told that among his people, the Mandingo, "Juba" was someone evil – up to no good. Juba is an African word. Bessie Jones said that when she learned it as a child she learned it as "gibba" not "juba," and "gibba" came from giblets. With poultry "gibba" is the gizzard, the heart, the liver, and the feet; with the pig, "gibba" is the tongue, the snout, the ears, the neckbones, the chitterlings, the feet, and the tail – those parts of the foodstuffs that were least valued. Gibba (giblets) became the basis of the diet slaves had to eat. Jones would use the word as a noun and as a verb. She often said in explanation of the term, "You just gibba me, you gibba me this and gibba that and if you had to take it, it would kill you." Meaning? You reserve for me what you think are the worst parts of everything!

You sift the meal and give me the husk
You cook the bread and give me the crust
You eat the meat and give me the skin
And that's where my mama's trouble begin.

Then there is a part of the play where everyone is up doing what Bessie Jones called the "scissors":

Juba up! Juba down! Juba all around the town
Just! Juba! Juba! Juba this and Juba that
Juba killed the yellow cat
Bent over double-trouble Juba!

Bessie Jones said that the dance that people today call the "charleston" they called the "scissors." It was when White people started to dance it that the name changed to the charleston. Within this one song, there are several stories: the survival and evolution of drumming and rhythms in African American culture; protesting the everyday trouble of slavery through complaints about the allocation of foodstuffs; a word that is African, "juba," was also understood as a word in an English context, "gibba," and used as a verb and a noun; and a dance that is called one thing among the Black community being renamed when it crosses over into White social dance practice.

Bessie Jones called "Juba" a "play." Mrs. Jones used the terms "play," "game," and "dance" differently. In her introduction to a collection of Bessie Jones's children's repertoire, ethnomusicologist Bess Lomax Hawes wrote:

When they [the Sea Islanders] "played" they were constructing over and over again small life-dramas; they were improvising on the central issues of their deeper concerns; they were taking on new personalities for identification or caricature: they were acting. . . . [The plays] are ceremonials, small testimonies to the ongoingness of life, not miniature battles. In order to be enjoyed properly, therefore, they must be done properly – that is joyfully and humorously but with an underlying seriousness of intent to make it all come out right, to make, as Mrs. Jones says so often and so touchingly, "a beautiful play."[5]

Plays always had a story or a message, something that could teach you how to live. It was from Bessie Jones that I learned the "play" she called "Mama Lama Cuma Lama." In this play, one got a chance to lead, to follow, and to work in a group with all of the other players.

Mama lama cuma lama cuma la bisa!
Mama lama cuma lama cuma la bisa!
Oh no no no no la bisa!
Oh no no no no la bisa!

This part is done by everyone. We all stand in a circle, and we sing the chorus together, in harmony if we know how. And we clap our own hands to make our own sound, and then clap the hands of our neighbors to make the sound of the group. We can move our feet and the rest of our bodies any way we want as long as keep the song going, and clap our hands and our neighbors' hands at the right time. Then we sing:

Enny eeny desa deeny ooh la thumba leeny
Achy kachy libba rachy XYZ!
Eeny meeny desa deeny ooh la thum ba leeny
Achy kachy libba rachy XYZ!

During this part the person who is "it" jumps to the center of the circle and does a dance or step, and during the second set of lines everybody in the circle does the same step that "it" has created. As the leader you must be creative, because you have to make up your step and not copy anybody else. While you are "it" everybody else follows your lead. In the next moment you, the leader, are back in the circle, having chosen another player to be "it." Back in the circle with the group, you do the group section together; when the "it" part comes around, you, the previous leader, now follow someone else's lead.

Bessie Jones taught us that games and plays were fun, but plays also taught people how to live with each other. I really identified with the part of the plays in which one was positioned to make up something new. When it came your turn to be "it," you were the temporary leader. Notice the absence of gender. As a leader in real life, you have to create your own path sometimes. In this play you are stimulated to create, to come up with something you have never done before, and the next minute you are looking at everybody else doing what you came up with. I liked that the leader was always changing – that one minute you are leading, and the next minute you are back in the chorus and the group is thundering together with no special lead sticking out. The next minute there is another leader, but it is not you – it is someone else, and now you are the follower.

The position in the play of "it" always reminded me of how much I heard older people talking about "a way out of no way." This line showed up in prayers and conversations and always pointed to God and spirit working in your life in situations where there was no way out that you could see. And if you found that you still came up with something that got you through, then that was "a way out of no way." It seemed to me that this play drilled us as children to open that part of ourselves that could come up with something new.

Bessie Jones also provided new ways for me to think about being a woman in this world. As a female, her story was such a link to the slavery we had survived, and it provided other options to understanding and defining morality and integrity when it came to sexual practices. We have her words because of the work of John Stewart, who took down her autobiography and published it in 1982, and to him we owe a great debt. In telling the story of her lineage, she goes down the line of her mother and her mother's mother.

The women in Bessie Jones's family did not always marry. They did not think that marriage was the natural goal for a woman. The women in her family seemed to view sex as a natural practice that began when your body became opened to it. Bessie Jones's first child was born when she was twelve. While sharing this story, she also spoke about how to carry oneself and take care of oneself with respect. Having a child out of wedlock did not automatically mean one was loose and undeserving of respect. And having a child out of wedlock did not in itself amount to the sin I had been taught about.

In my community, when a girl got pregnant out of wedlock, she had "messed up." She had sinned, and if she was a member of the church she was "unchurched," or put out of the church. After the baby was born, the mother had to come before the congregation and beg the church pardon before they would restore her back to being a member in good standing. I never saw a man put out of the church because he had fathered a child out of wedlock. I never saw a man beg the church pardon because of sex. I hated the rule! It was refreshing to find in Bessie Jones a religious woman who had worked out something else about righteousness in this world.

Having her first child when she was twelve felt too early for me, but I saw something of what we had to do as women and people evolving out of a slavery system where sex was forced, chosen, coerced, sought after, as well as rejected. But when a woman or girl-woman became pregnant, she was surrounded with as much support as the other women could provide.

For me, growing up in a house where my mother was strict about sexual morals, I learned that I was in a church where God was directly concerned with who, when, and how one had sex, and it was not supposed to happen until after marriage – at least for women. It was amazing to be around and listen to Mrs. Jones, an older woman who came out of a tradition fashioned by the realities of slavery and taking the whole sphere of sexual practice in a softer, more open and gentle way, with more support and less disdain for the women who for whatever reason moved into motherhood outside of marriage. Jones talked with Stewart about the women in her life:

> My name is Mary Elizabeth, and I'm named after Momma's mother and Momma's grandma. Momma's mother was named Elizabeth and her grandmother Mary, I'm named after both of them.
>
> Now I don't know if Mary [Bessie Jones's great-grandmother] had any husband or not, but Elizabeth [her grandmother], she didn't have one. She had eight children, though, and I remember some of them. I remember Aunt Evaline, and Lutecia, and Robert – the one they called Son

that got lynched – Momma, and I don't remember the rest of them. My mother before she married went by the name of Roberts, but she was Green. There was a man named Bill Green – they just called him Green – he was the daddy of Momma and Uncle Robert; but I don't know who the daddy for the rest of my grandmother's children were.[6]

There was so much of this recounting of her family's parentage that came from the legacy of slavery, where fatherhood often disappeared – because to have it acknowledged would also involve naming White men, who fathered children with slave women under their control. African Americans moved beyond slavery, engaging in a struggle to reconstruct families, and in many cases, partnering in marriage took hold. But sometimes for many reasons African American men fathered children but did not raise them. "Being there no matter what" became the realm of African American women and those who supported and encouraged them. Jones let us know that sometimes African American women chose not to marry, even as they began to create a family:

Elizabeth, my grandmother, never was married. She never did marry, but she had her share of children. My momma say I took after her, 'cause I didn't never want to marry. Never wanted to marry, I didn't prefer marrying. My momma say that's the way her mother was. Say she didn't look for no marriage at all. She had her freedom. And then when she had it, she finished righteous. Told them, say, "You see where God don't care nothing about that little stuff you do?"

You see, the Lord don't care nothing about that stuff. What

I'm saying is that all those things like that didn't send my grandmother to hell 'cause she didn't marry a man.[7]

This was one of the first times I heard an elder say that God and Jesus were not personally involved with sexual practices. That to have a child and not marry did not in and of itself send you to hell. It was a refreshing breath of fresh air in a stagnant, church-based dialogue on morals with little accounting for the sexually pressured reality of girls' and women's lives. Bessie Jones's grandmother's life revealed that sometimes those of us who survived slavery came into freedom bearing scars that shaped the way we looked at freedom and independence. Here was a story of women who believed that the God they served knew them and their hearts and was flexible on motherhood and marriage during slavery and freedom. And this woman, to be free and independent, decided it was important not to marry anybody. Bessie Jones felt that she had a model in the choices of her grandmother:

> She raised her children, she did them well. . . . So I would've thought that too. I could raise my chillun, and I couldn't raise my man, see. I don't think I ever would have married if I hadn't wanted to go on and live for the Lord, and I knew since I was a singer, and being the way I was with people, friendly, they would accuse me of every man that came by. I didn't want to be slurred all the time, so I thought I better go ahead and get my own husband. That's the only reason I married, and that's the truth. Course I liked him alright, but I wouldn't have married him. I would have gone on. But after you've decided to live your life in the church, and you're a grown woman, you need your own husband.[8]

Jones negotiates the territory between what she believes to be true and the reality of living in a church-based community, traveling as a woman and interacting with church folk – female and male. She decided that in order to be in the church and to be a singer, she had to be married so that her reputation would not be slurred. The decision was not spiritually based, it was social, cultural, and political.

Having the chance to work with someone who was intimate with the nineteenth century and who cherished the knowledge she carried from her parents and grandparents made me more interested in what I had within me that had been passed by those older than me. It was also important to know someone who threaded her life through what she had been taught by her family and the contemporary realities she faced that made her sometimes choose differently from those around her.

Learning from Bessie Jones and reclaiming what I had from slavery led me to examine more closely the lives of Sojourner Truth and Harriet Tubman. They had come to me as a young child and very much as if they were two sisters. At first I could not separate them. As I grew older, I began to sort out the stories – Harriet Tubman was a conductor on the Underground Railroad and Sojourner was a great preacher who spoke out against slavery and for women's rights, and said what she thought anywhere she thought it. We all grew up on the story of her baring her breast in a public meeting where she was speaking when a heckler suggested that she must be a man. I came to understand that both of these women, who had been a part of my psychic strength since I was a young child, were also singers, often fashioning their songs to fit a particular need.

Learning more about these two nineteenth-century women helped me to understand the tradition of singing and fighting for justice and the idea of a stage being wherever the struggle is at the time. Sojourner Truth was known for her sermons and her speeches. When she preached, she would often also sing, and some of the songs were created by her. My favorite is a song called "The Valient Soldiers" set to the tune of "John Brown's Body." Truth created this song in tribute to the Colored Regiment from Michigan who went into the Civil War as Union soldiers. I was so thrilled to discover these lyrics and, with slight text adjustments for accessibility to contemporary audiences, was moved to include it in the repertoire of Sweet Honey In The Rock:

> We are (the valient) colored Yankee soldiers
> Enlisted for the war
> We are fighting for the union
> We are fighting for the law
> We can shoot a Rebel further
> Than a White man ever saw
> As we go marching on.

> Look there above the center
> Where the flag is waving bright
> We are going out of slavery
> We are bound for freedom's light
> We mean to show Jeff Davis
> How the Africans can fight
> As we go marching on.

> We are done with hoeing cotton
> We are done with hoeing corn

We are colored Yankee soldiers
Just as sure as you are born
When the Rebels hear us shouting
They will think it's Gabriel's horn
As we go marching on.

They will have to pay us wages
The wages of their sins
They will have to bow their foreheads
To their colored kith and kin
They'll have to give us house room
Or the roofs will tumble in
As we go marching on.

We be as the Proclamation
Rebels hush it as you will
The birds will sing it to us
Hopping on the cotton hills
The possum up the gum tree
Couldn't keep it still
As we go marching on.

Now Abraham has spoken
And the message has been sent
The prison doors are opened
And out the prisoners went
To join the Sable Army
Of African descent
As we go marching on.

Glory Glory Hallelujah
Glory Glory Hallelujah

Glory Glory Hallelujah
As we go marching on.[9]

The intensity and sharpness of voice and stance expressed in this text made me revise my understanding of Sojourner Truth. This song also brought me closer to the fierceness with which African Americans endeavored to fight in the Civil War. There is no question in this text about the cause of the war, where the side of righteousness rested, and the importance of the African American contribution to the effort.

Sojourner Truth was not born to this state of being a radical, politically minded songmaker and speaker. She was not born Sojourner; she was born into slavery and lived her early years cooperating with the system – she had to create the Sojourner I was introduced to as a child. Sojourner had been named Isabella and was born in Ulster County, the Dutch farming region of New York, between 1797 and 1800. She was the daughter of James and Elizabeth (also called Betsy and Mau Mau Bett). Her father was also called Bomefree – the Dutch word for "tree." They were the slaves of Colonel Johannis Hardenbergh. When he died, the family became the property of his son, Charles, who built a hotel with a large one-room cellar where all the slaves lived.[10]

In her narrative, written down by Gilbert Olive and published in 1850, Sojourner described this cellar as damp and dark, with a few panes of glass through which the sun never shone. The floorboards were loose, and the space beneath was filled with mud and water. Her parents had had ten or twelve children, Isabella and her brother Peter being the youngest. Isabella's older sisters and brothers were all sold before she got to know them. She did remember well the selling of her sister Nancy, aged three, and her brother Michael, aged five, while she was still an infant. She remembered because over and over she heard her mother and father tell the story of losing their young children to the slave trade.

Her family spoke Dutch, and Sojourner knew no English before she was ten. When she was nine, her master died and she was sold to a Mr. Neeley. She received countless beatings because she knew no English. She asked God to send her her father – he came, and she asked her father to help her find another master. She was shortly afterward sold to a fisherman and tavern owner named Scriver.

Reading her narrative, I found myself drawn to her childhood fluency with God. She got her first images of God from her mother, Mau Mau Bett, who told her that there would be those times when the only one she could turn to was God, and that she could go to God and tell him about her troubles and he would not leave her alone. Isabella took this literally, and, knowing God was a long way off, she would go away by herself where she couldn't be heard by those on the plantation. She had a special place by a stream where the water would cover the sound of her voice and she would tell God out loud what was happening to her. She would also tell God what she wanted done about her condition and strike deals with God. If God would take care of her situation, she would do something on her side of the proposed agreement. Situations like praying to God to send her father when she was being beaten, and having that result in a change of masters, reinforced her belief in her relationship: "Though it seems curious, I do not remember ever asking for anything but what I got it. And I always received it as an answer to my prayers. When I got beaten, I never knew it long enough beforehand to pray; and I always thought if I only had had time to pray to God for help, I should have escaped this beating."[11] As Sojourner Truth, she traded in this earlier practice as she grew in her understanding of conventional prayer and worship communication with God. For myself, I missed the earlier child dialogues and contracts with God.

When she was about twelve, Isabella was sold again, this time to John J. Dumont, with whom she spent the rest of her time as a slave. During this time, she had five children with Thomas, another slave on the plantation. She was a hard worker, actually overexerting herself so much so that she was not well liked by other slaves on the plantation because of the amount of work she did. She did not at this time question the system of slavery.

At some point Isabella decided that she wanted to be a slave no longer. She was able to make an arrangement with Dumont whereby he agreed that after one more year of work, he would grant her freedom. Sometime during what was to be her last year as a slave, she injured her hand. When it came time that the year was up, Dumont told her that because of that injury, she had not given him a year's worth of work. Isabella thought that, on any day in any week, she was doing twice as much as anybody else, and that even with an injured hand she was pulling her load. To be fair, however, she stayed several months past the agreed date to be sure she had carried out her share of the contract.

After Isabella felt certain that she had more than fulfilled her share of the contract with Dumont, she decided that she would just leave and that she would not run in her leaving. She walked off this plantation early one morning late in 1826 just as the sun was rising, with a baby in her arms. She was led to the family of Isaac and Maria Van Wagener. When Dumont came for her and her baby, the Van Wageners, who were opposed to the buying and selling of humans, paid $25.00 to cover Sojourner's labors for the rest of the year and an additional $5.00 for her child. Isabella then took the name of Wagener, her last master in the eyes of the law, who secured her freedom and the freedom of her child.

The New York law abolishing slavery went into effect July 4, 1827. However, the law did not change the status of all slaves immediately – only slaves born before 1799 would be free. There was a process written into the law whereby if one was a slave of a certain age, one would still owe one's master more years of service. Many people had to stay on plantations after this date because of a recipe that required service years after slavery was abolished. Isabella's children owed Dumont time, and, except for her baby, she left them there.

In 1827, she found out that her son Peter, who was one of the children she left on the plantation when she took her freedom, had been sold to a Dr. Solomon Gedney, one of Dumont's (Peter's master's) in-laws. Through a series of events, Peter ended up being shipped south to an Alabama planter named Fowler, who had married Solomon Gedney's sister Eliza. It was against New York State law, which prohibited the sale of slaves outside of the state. When Isabella heard that her son had been shipped to Alabama, she went for help. She was determined to get her son back! Her response showed that when she left her children, she did not leave her children. The tie was not severed. She made up her mind that she was going to get her son back.

She went first to her former mistress, Mrs. Dumont, and then to Mrs. Gedney, the mother of Eliza Gedney Fowler, the bride who was now in her new home in Alabama with Sojourner's son Peter. In turn, Isabella asked these women why had they allowed her son to be sent to Alabama. In her narrative, it is recounted that Mrs. Dumont responded, "Ugh, a fine fuss to make about a little Nigger!! . . . Making such a halloo-balloo about the neighborhood; and all for a paltry nigger!!!" Isabella answered, "I'll have my son again!" Mrs. Gedney, the bride's mother, told Isabella, "Dear me! What a disturbance to make about your child! What, is your child better than my child?" Isabella said, "Yes, your child has gone there, but she is married and my boy has gone there, but he is a slave, and he is too young to go so far from his mother. Oh, I must have my child!"[12]

I remember first reading the account of these scenes and slowly realizing that these women did not see Isabella as a mother and did not see Peter as her son. Peter was a slave and property to be moved around as his owners saw fit. Neither woman identified with or was touched by this mother's capacity for love and grief. Mrs. Gedney, the mother of the bride, seemed shocked to find that this Black woman thought her child's state was worse than her daughter's. Isabella left knowing that she would not find any assistance from these mothers. Her sense of loss would not penetrate the barrier they carried inside them and kept her outside of any experience they could have. The curtain of race and slavery was too thick for women to get together over their shared experiences as mothers separated from their children. These women could not relate to Isabella's desire to have her child back.

Isabella found help among her Quaker friends, who responded to her plea and told her she had to go to the courthouse and tell the grand jury. Sojourner thought that "grand jury" was someone's name. When she finally made it to the room where she could be heard, she told her story and got legal support. And step by step, Isabella would not let go. There was no end to how far this mother would go to get her son back. The day came for Peter to be brought back to the state of New York and into the courtroom to finally be returned to his mother. However, in the process of getting Peter back, the master had turned Peter against Isabella, and in the courtroom Peter rejected her. It took a while before he would get out of that courtroom with his mother.

Historian Nell Irwin Painter, who has written a biography of Sojourner, also has an article about what she refers to as "soul murder."[13] She writes about the fact that there is a cost that is paid when one is abused, raped, beaten, and repeatedly violated. Even if you survive the violence, there is a way in which your soul can be distorted or destroyed. Sometimes, if you are not alone, if there are others who can surround you with understanding, the damage is lessened. She wants us to know that we do not as a people move through slavery into freedom unscarred. Being a part of a supportive community gives one a better chance of not continuing the cycle of violence. Isabella and her son were victims of the violence of slavery.[14]

One of the points that Painter makes is that a batterer who whips Black people day in and day out is a danger to anybody. Our culture has three hundred years of this openly sanctioned activity of beating slaves to control them. Slavery was a national phenomenon, even though we like to think of it as regional – beating people who are less powerful than you is a part of the national culture. When Isabella examined Peter, she found that he had scars all over his body. He told her that sometimes he was beaten every day and would hide under the steps. The bride Eliza Fowler was his only source of relief, she would sometimes wait until night and then would find him and put salves on his wounds. When Isabella saw the scars, she said, "Oh, Lord Jesus, Look! See my poor child! Oh Lord, render them double, for all this!"[15] Some time later, Isabella heard that this Fowler, this evil planter, had beaten his wife Eliza to death. Isabella recalled the prayer she had breathed in her time of rage over the brutality that her son had received and was horrified at the possibility that she had through her anguish been a factor in this tragic death.[16]

Isabella's walking off the plantation did not immediately make her the fighter I had been taught about. She moved to New York and became involved in a small religious cult community where, socially, she was on the bottom of the group, working and serving everyone. When cult members were brought into court because of the suspicious death of one of their members, Isabella was included in the list of those charged. However, again she was able to get legal help and was cleared of all charges.

She left New York on June 1, 1843, headed east, and changed her name to Sojourner Truth to match her new work and mission. I have often thought about the name Sojourner Truth and about this woman naming herself by her work. She was now committing her life to first being a wandering preacher, moving around and speaking the truth as she experienced it through the Holy Spirit.

One of the earliest stories about her use of singing occurred early in the years of her life and work as Sojourner Truth. She had the occasion of using a song to quell riotous behavior that threatened to destroy a camp meeting in a field in Northampton, Massachusetts. When she began to sing, the men disrupting the meeting shifted and began to quiet down and listen to her. The song was a hymn she had composed, "It Was Early in the Morning":

It was early in the morning
It was early in the morning
Just as the break of day
When he rose and went to heaven on a cloud.[17]

It became one of her favorite songs and is said to be the last one she sang just before she died.

During the 1840s and 1850s Sojourner could be found speaking against slavery and for women's rights and temperance. The Abolitionist Movement created many songs whose lyrics addressed the wrongs of holding people in bondage. In most cases they were sung to tunes that were in popular usage as hymns or secular songs. One of the songs Sojourner created about the traumas of slavery was to the tune of "Auld Lang Syne":

I am pleading for my people,
A poor downtrodden race
Who dwell in freedom's boasted land
With no abiding place.

I am pleading for the mothers
Who gaze in wild despair
Upon the hated auction block
And see their children there.

Whilst I bear upon my body
The scars of many a gash
I am pleading for my people
Who groan beneath the lash.[18]

In 1865, at the end of the Civil War, Sojourner was in Washington DC working in Freedman's Hospital. During this time, she directly opposed segregated practices on street trolleys. There was one car called the Jim Crow car on each track, where Blacks would usually have to stand because Whites had the seats. Sojourner complained to the president of the street railroad, and the Jim Crow car was taken off. Then the trolley conductors would not pick her up. On one occasion, she shouted, "I want to ride!" The car stopped and she jumped aboard. Another time, she chased the car down.[19] It was also during this time that she decided that her people needed to be on their own land and not in refugee camps living off the government.[20] As a woman, she believed that women had as much right to the vote as men and that to give only men the vote would mean that there would then be another way for a man to have power over a woman. She was such a force to contend with. No wonder she still walks through the twenty-first century!!

My earliest images of Harriet Tubman are clearer than my images of Sojourner Truth. She came to me with a song we sang in school and a story about her fighting for the freedom of our people during slavery. When I learned the spiritual "Wade in the Water," I was told that it was a Harriet Tubman song and that she used it when she was a conductor on the Underground Railroad, urging our people to go on even when times got hard and obstacles seemed threatening:

Wade in the water, wade in the water children
Wade in the water, God's gonna trouble the water.

See those children dressed in white
The leader looks like that Israelite.

See those children dressed in red

They look like the children that Moses led.

See those children dressed in blue
They look like my people marching through.

Some say Peter and some say Paul
Ain' but the one God made us all.

Some come cripple and some come lame
But I come stepping in Jesus name.

This song comes from the Bible story about Jesus coming to the pool of Bathzatha (Bethesda or Bethsaida), in Jerusalem. In John 5:2–9, one finds the story:

> Now there is in Jerusalem by the Sheep Gate a pool, in Hebrew called Bathzatha, which has five porticoes. In these lay a multitude of invalids, blind, lame, paralyzed; waiting for the moving of the water. For an angel of the Lord went down at certain seasons into the pool and troubled the water, whoever stepped in first after the troubling of the water was healed of whatever disease he had. One man was there, who had been ill for thirty-eight years. When Jesus saw him and knew that he had been lying there a long time, he said to him, "Do you want to be healed?" The sick man answered him, "Sir, I have no man to put me into the pool when the water is troubled, and while I am going, another steps down before me." Jesus said to him, "Rise, take up your pallet and walk." And at once the man was healed, and he took up his pallet and walked.

As a child, when I heard ministers, including my father, preach from this passage, they focused on the section where Jesus heals the crippled man. However, the text of the spiritual "Wade in the Water" centers on the concept of "troubled water" that, once charged by the power of Spirit, has the power to transform and heal. The song said to us, then and now, go ahead, get in the water.

As a child I pondered this song because it had an upbeat, soft swing to it. It felt as if it was saying to go ahead into something that was trouble. My parents, my teacher, all adults around me who loved and cared about me told me over and over again to stay away from trouble. So what was this song that I had learned from these same people that said that trouble was okay to go into, that it was all right to risk your life and put yourself in trouble? It took my own living to answer the question. It was not until I found myself in a situation where I could choose between an immediate safety and an action that would endanger me that I understood that often, if you want to be changed or healed or to be different, you cannot always steer around trouble. Sometimes you have to go through trouble. When I went on my first march in Albany, Georgia, I moved outside of the safety zone and walked through troubled waters – God-troubled waters – and I have never been the same since. Of course, moving through dangers, one is not guaranteed freedom or life. You strike out for freedom and transformation, knowing only that you must leave where you are.

When you move from the plantation in your life, you must also work to leave the plantation you hold inside. Survival on the plantation is connected to your agreeing in some limited way to be bound by its rules. When you decide to leave, you must be ready to leave that part of yourself that has moved in these old ways. In a way, that part of you must die. It would not do to move to the other side, to travel the journey with Harriet, to get to the land beyond slavery, and then find that you have taken the mindset of the plantation with you.

Who was Harriet Tubman, and how did she come to be this extraordinary woman? Who was this woman, the first I had ever heard called by two powerful names associated with males – Moses and General? Harriet Tubman was born into slavery in 1820 and named Araminta Ross. Her family lived on the plantation of Edward Broadus in Dorchester County, Maryland. She was one of eleven children of Harriet Green and Benjamin Ross. She later adopted her mother's name. Araminta was hired or farmed out at the age of six to the farm of James Cook to be taught to weave, and she was also in charge of the muskrat traps that were underwater. Even when she was sick with the measles, she was sent to tend the traps. As a result she became extremely ill. She was sent back by Cook to her mother, who slowly nursed her back to health, only to be farmed out again. This cycle was repeated several times with her being farmed out and worked and beaten until too sick to work, back to her mother's to be nursed, and then out again. When she was twelve, she demanded to be sent to the fields. She never wanted to work inside the plantation house again.[21]

At thirteen, Araminta witnessed the overseer following a man, also a slave named Barrett, who slipped away from the plantation. When I first read this, I knew right away that she was going to follow the overseer. I don't know if you have the experience of reading and you see trouble coming. In my mind I started to talk to Araminta. "Do you know what you are doing? You are going to get in trouble!!" True enough, when she got to the store at the village square, the overseer had already grabbed the man and was trying to get others to help him hold him. The fleeing man broke away and ran. As he ran through the door, the overseer picked up a two-pound weight and threw it just as Araminta stepped in the door. The weight hit her in the head. She was taken back to her mother again, unconscious, and this time it was thought she would not survive. Again her mother nursed her through a long recovery. However, as a result of this injury, Araminta had a permanent dent in her skull and suffered from Blackout spells. Despite this injury, Harriet lived a long time.[22]

I remember another version of the same story as told to me by my teacher. In this version, Harriet was in a field, and the overseer picked up a rock to stop a man making a run for freedom: Harriet stepped in and took the blow meant for the fleeing slave. In this version, the action felt impulsive. However, in the story Harriet tells to Sarah Bradford, from the time she followed the overseer she was committed to becoming involved. I have to keep telling myself her age to understand that we are talking about a young girl, just entering her young womanhood.

Then there are the things that go around in my head when I am reading about her following the overseer. It is clear that I know that there is going to be trouble, but what comes up is not an understanding of the movement toward "transforming trouble" referred to in the "Wade in the Water" spiritual. The song does say "Wade in the Water" – go ahead, there is going to be trouble, if you want change – go ahead. And when I think about Harriet Tubman, I think she was born in trouble and moved very early to being willing to chance trouble that might kill or free her. Harriet Tubman's life is one of a force seeking the paths that would draw risk and trouble, but it also provided a chance for freedom.

In 1844 Harriet, in her twenties, married a free Black man named John Tubman. After five years, she heard that because her master was dead, some of the slaves might be auctioned off to pay off his debts. Harriet and two of her brothers were whispered to be on the list. In her narrative, Harriet Tubman tells of a vision she had during this time:

> And in the visions of the night she saw the horsemen coming, and heard the shrieks of women and children, as they were being torn from each other, and hurried off no one knew whither.
>
> And beckoning hands were ever motioning her to come, and she seemed to see a line dividing the land of slavery from the land of freedom, and on the other side of that line she saw lovely White ladies waiting to welcome her, and to care for her. Already in her mind her people were the Israelites in the land of Egypt, while far away to the north somewhere, was the land of Canaan.[23]

Harriet and her two brothers decided to leave the plantation. In her narrative Harriet says that the brothers started with her but decided to return to the plantation, giving Harriet their blessings and returning to what they knew. In her leaving, singing comes up again, for as she moved across the yard and through the slave quarters she sang this song:

> *When dat ar ole chariot comes*
> *I'm gwine to lebe you*
> *I'm bound for the promised land*
> *Friends I'm gwine to lebe you.*
>
> *I'm sorry friends to lebe you*
> *Farewell, oh fare thee well*
> *But I'll meet you in de morning*
> *Fare thee well oh fare thee well.*

I'll meet you in de morning
When you reach de promised land
On the other side of Jordan
For I'm bound for de promised land.[24]

After she was gone, her song was remembered for a long time back on the plantation. She had sung it to say goodbye and to let her people know that she was gone. I can imagine them recalling the words of the last song they had heard her sing as they began to understand that she was now gone. They used the song, which they pulled out of their minds and hearts and sang to themselves, whenever they wondered where she was and how she was.

Harriet reaches from the nineteenth century to me as a twentieth-and twenty-first-century singer and shows me another kind of stage for singing songs and another kind of listening: where you can hear a song, enjoy it for what is understood at that time and in that moment. Then, there is a future time when you have changed or your situation has changed, and the song releases another message. Songs and singing become a part of your life and are so twisted and twined up with everything in your life that as you move you can glean more of what they hold.

During the Civil Rights Movement, in jail, I discovered that different songs at different times in different situations came up for me. These were songs I had sung all my life. Now they were mine to sing together with all the women in that jail cell, and by singing we could hold out for a little while longer. At the time I learned the songs and while I sang them in church service and school, I never guessed that, in jail – changed by my choice to join the Movement – they could voice what I was becoming and, one day, I would know so much more about them.

As children we were told that in her work with the Underground Railroad, Tubman always carried a gun and never allowed anyone to change her or his mind. I have wondered in my mind if that additional insurance had to do with her first experience, knowing that when you run sometimes fear would pull you back. Harriet made that first journey alone. How did she persevere? She had worked out for herself who she was in the world, and that became her license for the life she began to lead. "I had reasoned dis out in my mind; there was one of two things I had a right to, liberty, or death; if I could not have one, I would have de oder; for no man should take me alive; I should fight for my liberty as long as my strength lasted, and when de time came for me to go, de Lord would let dem take me."[25]

When Harriet left the plantation, she left alone, but there is a story that she told to a Boston journalist of a White woman who helped her on her journey.[26] There were a growing number of people, Black and White, who were willing to risk their safety to help slaves to freedom. Finally, Harriet Tubman arrived in Philadelphia a free woman. For her the world had changed: "I looked at my hands to see if I was the same person, now that I was free. There was such a glory over everything."[27]

After working to save money, she returned to Maryland to get her husband, but he had remarried. It is said that she made nineteen journeys south to lead slaves, including all her living brothers and sisters and aged parents, to freedom. She never took the same route twice, and she maintained strict discipline among her followers. Harriet Tubman is our most well-known conductor on the Underground Railroad. Her Philadelphia contact was William Still, who described her as one who "in point of courage, shrewdness and disinterested exertions to rescue her fellow-men, by making personal visits to Maryland among the slaves . . . was without her equal."[28] Still also noted that Tubman sometimes worked with the Quaker and abolitionist Thomas Garrett of Wilmington, Delaware. In a letter, Garrett wrote: "We made arrangements last night, and sent away Harriet Tubman, with six men and one woman to Allen Agnew's to be forwarded across the country to the city. Harriet, and one of the men had worn their shoes off their feet, and I gave them two dollars to help fit them out, and directed a carriage to be hired at my expense, to take them out."[29]

Both Harriet and Sojourner sang this next song, whose existence is based on the passage of the Fugitive Slave Act of 1850. This act meant that Black people who had successfully escaped to the North could be brought back and that any citizen could be deputized to assist planters or their representatives in seizing fugitive slaves. The northern states were no longer safe. "After that, I couldn't trust Uncle Sam wived my people no longer, but I brought em all clar off to Canada."[30]

I'm on my way to Canada
That cold and dreary land
De sad effects of slavery
I can't no longer stand.

I've served my master all my days
Without a dime reward
And now I'm forced to run away
To flee the lash, abroad.

Faretheewell, ole Master
Don't think hard of me
I'm traveling on to Canada

Where all the slaves are free.

De hounds are baying on my tracks
Ole Master comes behind
Resolved that he will bring me back
Before I cross the line.

I'm now embarked for yonder shore
Where a man's a man by law
De iron horse will bear me o'er,
To shake de lion paw.

Oh righteous father
Wilt thou not pity me
And help me on to Canada
Where all the slaves are free.

Oh I heard Queen Victoria say
That if we would forsake
Our native land of slavery
And come across de lake.

Dat she was standing on de shore
Wived arms extended wide
To give us all a peaceful home,
Beyond de rolling tide.

Faretheewell, ole master,
Don't think hard of me,
I'm traveling on to Canada
Where all de slaves are free.[31]

Tubman's work was extremely dangerous and against the law.
There was a "dead or alive" warrant on her head; rewards at one

point reached $40,000, but she never lost a passenger. When Harriet would leave her band to scout ahead, she would come back signaling with a song:

Hail, oh hail, ye happy spirits
Death no more shall make you fear
Grief nor sorrow, pain nor anguish
Shall no more distress you dere.

Around Him are ten thousand angels
Always ready to obey command
Dey are always hovering round you
Till you reach de heavenly land.

Jesus, Jesus will go wived you
He will lead you to his throne
He who died, has gone before you,
Trod de wine-press all alone.

He whose thunders shake creation
He who bids de planets roll
He who rides upon the tempest
And whose scepter sways de whole.

Dark and thorny is the pathway
Where the pilgrim makes his ways
But beyond dis vale of sorrow
Lie de fields of endless days.[32]

According to Bradford, taking down this story, "The air sung to these words was so wild, so full of plaintive miner strains and unexpected quavers, that I would defy any White person to learn it, and often as I heard it, it was to be a constant surprise."[33]

"Go Down Moses" was a song she used to signal that the way was clear. It was a song that was not sung openly among her people in the South. It may have been the use of this song that gained her the name "Moses."

Oh go down, Moses
Way down into Egypt's land
Tell old Pharaoh
Let my people go.

Oh Pharaoh said he would go cross
Let my people go
And in de wilderness children don't get lost
Let my people go.

You may hinder me here, but you can't up dere,
He sits in Hebben and answers prayer.[34]

And then she would enter the area of the hiding place and they would continue on their journey another night.

Harriet Tubman met John Brown in Ontario, Canada, and was in support of the raid on the federal arsenal at Harper's Ferry, although she did not go because of illness. In the spring of 1860, while stopping in Troy, New York, she got involved with the struggle to free a fugitive slave who had been recaptured and was being reclaimed by his master, who was also his half-brother. Charles Nalle, the fugitive, looked as White as his younger half-brother, who was his master. His master brought the full forces of the law to have his property returned. Harriet was in the room when the decision came that Nalle would be returned. As the marshals took him down, Harriet got between Nalle and the Marshall and demanded to the crowd to kill them both rather than turn him over to the authorities. There ensued a battle that went on down to and across a river and ended up with Harriet seriously bruised. But she would not stop; she continued to look for ways to fight.[35]

During the Civil War, on the recommendation of the governor of Massachusetts, Tubman was hired by the United States Army Intelligence Department in Beaufort, South Carolina, to spy on Confederate encampments and relay messages on Southern strategy to Union officers. She also served as a nurse, tending the wounded and sick soldiers. During a raiding attack along the Combahee River in South Carolina, Harriet Tubman took on the job of convincing Blacks on shoreline plantations to place their trust in Union forces and defect to freedom. Over eight hundred slaves were freed in this massive exodus.[36] When they were crowding to get on the boats, Harriet used this song to calm their fears and bring order until all were boarded:

> O all the whole creation in the East or in the West
> The glorious Yankee nation is the greatest and the best
> Come along! Come Along! Don't be alarmed
> Uncle Sam is rich enough to give you all a farm.[37]

After the Civil War, she raised money for schools for former slaves. She petitioned the U.S. Department of the Army for a pension for her services. She received no payment for her services during the war, and it was not until her eightieth birthday that she received a pension of $20 a month for the rest of her life. With this she founded a home for aged and destitute former slaves. She purchased twenty-five acres of property next to her home in Auburn, New York, as a community farm for poor people. The Harriet Tubman Home for Indigent Aged Negroes, later known as the Harriet Tubman Home for the Aged in Auburn, is now a national landmark. She died in Auburn on March 10, 1913, at the age of ninety-three. Harriet Tubman died in the twentieth century. When I found that date, it seemed that it brought her closer to me. My father was born in 1909. And Bessie Jones was born in 1902. We all breathed air in the same century as Harriet Tubman.

Sojourner Truth, Harriet Tubman, Bessie Jones – I come into my life and my singing as a woman who had the best models – singing mothers who were fighters, whose lives taught me another way to be in this world.

Notes

1. The phrase "well made-up mind" is from a traditional African American church song:

   I got a well made-up mind
   Church I got a well made-up mind
   I got a well made-up mind to serve the Lord.

2. Logan, *Betrayal of the Negro*, was originally published as *The Negro in American Life and Thought: The Nadir, 1877–1901* (1954).

3. "The Right of the citizens of the United States to vote shall not be denied or abridged by the United States or by any State on account of race, color, or previous condition of servitude." This amendment passed Congress in 1869 and was ratified by the states in 1870. Virginia, Georgia, Mississippi, and Texas were Southern states required to ratify the Fifteenth Amendment in order to be readmitted into the Union.

4. For a detailed study of this migration, see Painter, *Exodusters*.

1. TWENTIETH-CENTURY GOSPEL

1. For more on Tindley, see Reagon, "Searching for Tindley," 37–52. Also, in the same collection of essays see Boyer, "Charles Albert Tindley," 53–78. There is also a full-length biography of Tindley by Ralph Jones, *Charles Albert Tindley*.

2. Reagon, "Searching for Tindley."

3. Reagon, "The Evolution of a Freedom Song," 64–89.

4. Ballard, *One More Day's Journey*, 161.

5. Joe Williams, panelist at Smithsonian Conference on Thomas Andrew Dorsey, October 26, 1985, Conference documentation, Smithsonian Institution, National Museum of American History, Archives Center.

6. For more on Dorsey, see Michael W. Harris's full-length biography, *Rise of Gospel Blues*. Also see the two essays on Dorsey in Reagon, *We'll Understand It Better By and By*, section 4: Horace Clarence Boyer, "Take My Hand," 141–63; and Michael W. Harris, "Conflict and Resolution," 165–82.

7. Thomas Andrew Dorsey, as quoted on the radio show "Precious Lord: The Gospel Legacy of Thomas Andrew Dorsey," show 16 of the *Wade in the Water: African American Sacred Music Traditions* radio series, produced by National Public Radio and Smithsonian Institution, premier broadcast, January 1994. The audio quote was originally from an interview by Studs Terkel for the Studs Terkel Show, Radio Station WFMT, Chicago.

8. Boyer, "The Compositional Style of Thomas Andrew Dorsey."

9. Boyer, "Compositional Style of Thomas Andrew Dorsey."

10. Nierenberg, *Say Amen, Somebody*.

11. Boyer, "The Compositional Style of Roberta Martin."

12. Anderson, interview, *Wade in the Water* collection.

13. Reagon, "Kenneth Morris," 341. See also Boyer, "Kenneth Morris," 309–28.

14. Williams-Jones, "Roberta Martin," 255–74. For more on Martin see Boyer, "Roberta Martin," 275–86; and Williams-Jones and Reagon, "Conversations," 287–307.

15. Williams, *This Is My Story*, 23.

16. Williams, *This Is My Story*, 26–27.

17. Williams-Jones, "Afro-American Gospel Music," 380.

18. Smallwood, interview.

19. Smallwood, *Adoration*.

20. Cieply, *Stagebill*.

2. THE AFRICAN AMERICAN CONGREGATIONAL SONG TRADITION

1. This essay is based on a series of interviews conducted with Deacon Reardon between 1986 and 1993. The collection of interviews and recordings of prayer-band meetings are a part of the Bernice Johnson Reagon Archives, Washington DC.

2. In 1994 the Smithsonian Institution and National Public Radio (NPR) produced a twenty-six-part radio series entitled *Wade in the Water: African American Sacred Music Traditions*. Subsequent components included a Smithsonian traveling exhibition, a four-CD set (Smithsonian/Folkways), and a teacher curriculum guide (NPR).

3. SPIRITUALS

1. This essay is an adaptation and expansion of my program notes for "A Program of Spirituals," performed by Kathleen Battle and Jessye Norman at Carnegie Hall, New York, March 18, 1990, in *Stagebill, Carnegie Hall* (March 1990).

2. Roland Hayes, foreword to *My Songs*, vii.

3. Johnson and Johnson, *Book of American Negro Spirituals and Books of American Negro Spirituals*. A new paperback reprint was published by DaCapo Press, New York.

4. Douglass, *Narrative of the Life of Frederick Douglass*, 57–58.

5. Du Bois, "The Sorrow Songs," in *The Souls of Black Folk*, 197. The book was originally published in 1903.

6. Du Bois, "The Sorrow Songs," 197–98.

7. Jackson, *White Spirituals*, 273.

8. Brown, Davis, and Lee, *Negro Caravan*, 415–17.

9. Southern, *Music of Black Americans*, 96.

10. Southern, *Music of Black Americans*, 97.

11. Epstein, *Sinful Tunes and Spirituals*, 293–94.

12. Epstein, *Sinful Tunes and Spirituals*, 94.

13. Brown, Davis, and Lee, *Negro Caravan*, 413.

14. Epstein, *Sinful Tunes and Spirituals*, 259.

15. Du Bois, "The Sorrow Songs," 197.

16. Carter, interview.

17. Searles, interview.

18. Quoted in Turner, "Fisk Jubilee Singers," and Shockley, "Fisk Jubilee Singers."

19. Quoted in Turner, "Fisk Jubilee Singers," and Shockley, "Fisk Jubilee Singers."

20. Jesse Johnson, recorded audio statement.

21. Ann Elizabeth Wright, quoted in program dedication and welcome notice, by Helen R. Young and H. Tiajuana Malone, March 13, 1987, Albany GA, Katikati Cultural Center files.

22. Jesse Johnson, recorded audio statement.

23. McCree Harris, interview.

4. FREEDOM SONGS

1. Robeson, *The Spectator*, 86–87.

2. Du Bois, *Black Reconstruction in America*, 727.

3. Bessie Jones, *For the Ancestors*, 3.

4. During this same period, the constellation known as the Big Dipper, which points to the north star, was called the "drinking gourd." "Follow the Drinking Gourd" is a song about the Underground Railroad with some instructions for slaves striking out for freedom.

5. Bessie Jones and Bess Lomax Hawes, *Step It Down*, xv.

6. Bessie Jones, *For the Ancestors*, 3–4.

7. Bessie Jones, *For the Ancestors*, 4.

8. Bessie Jones, *For the Ancestors*, 4–5.

9. Truth, *Narrative*, 126, text adaptation as performed by Sweet Honey In The Rock.

10. For more on Sojourner Truth, see Gilbert, *Narrative of Sojourner Truth*, which is included in the expanded 1878 publication of her narrative with other materials. Two important contemporary biographies have been very important to my work on and with Truth's story: Mabee and Newhouse, *Sojourner Truth*, and Painter, *Sojourner Truth*.

11. Gilbert, *Narrative of Sojourner Truth*, 27.

12. Gilbert, *Narrative of Sojourner Truth*, 44–46.

13. Painter, "Soul Murder and Slavery," 125–46.

14. Painter, "Soul Murder and Slavery."

15. Gilbert, *Narrative of Sojourner Truth*, 54.

16. Gilbert, *Narrative of Sojourner Truth*, 55–58.

17. For more on Truth's work as a songwriter and singer, see Mabee and Newhouse, "Singer," *Sojourner Truth*, 219–31.

18. Mabee and Newhouse, *Sojourner Truth*, 227.

19. Truth, *Book of Life*, 184–86.

20. Truth, *Book of Life*, 199.

21. Bradford, *Harriet*, 108.

22. Bradford, *Harriet*, 109.

23. Bradford, *Harriet*, 26.

24. Bradford, *Harriet*, 28.

25. Bradford, *Harriet*, 29.

26. Bradford, *Harriet*, 111.

27. Bradford, *Harriet*, 30.

28. Still, *The Underground Railroad*, 305.

29. Still, *Underground Railroad*, 305.

30. Bradford, *Harriet*, 39.

31. Bradford, *Harriet*, 49–50.

32. Bradford, *Harriet*, 36–37.

33. Bradford, *Harriet*, 37.

34. Bradford, *Harriet*, 37–38.

35. Bradford, *Harriet*, 124–28. For more on the Nalle rescue, see Weise, *Troy's One Hundred Years*, 176–78.

36. Bradford, *Harriet*, 93–99.

37. Bradford, *Harriet*, 102.

Bibliography

Anderson, Robert. Interviewed by Bernice Johnson Reagon, Chicago IL, October 26, 1992. Audio recording and transcript, *Wade in the Water* collection, Smithsonian Institution, National Museum of American History, Archives Center.

Ballard, Allan. *One More Day's Journey: The Making of Black Philadelphia.* Philadelphia: Ishi Publications, 1987.

Boyer, Horace Clarence. "Charles Albert Tindley: Progenitor of African American Gospel Music." In Reagon, *We'll Understand It Better By and By.*

———. "The Compositional Style of Roberta Martin," Smithsonian Conference on Roberta Martin, February 1981, Conference documentation, Smithsonian Institution, National Museum of American History, Archives Center.

———. "The Compositional Style of Thomas Andrew Dorsey," Smithsonian Conference on Thomas Andrew Dorsey, October 26, 1985, Conference documentation, Smithsonian Institution, National Museum of American History, Archives Center.

———. "Kenneth Morris, Composer and Dean of Gospel Music Publishers." In Reagon, *We'll Understand It Better By and By.*

———. "Roberta Martin: Innovator of Modern Gospel Music." In Reagon, *We'll Understand It Better By and By.*

149

————. "Take My Hand, Precious Lord, Lead Me On." In Reagon, *We'll Understand It Better By and By*.

Bradford, Sarah H. *Harriet, the Moses of Her People*. 2nd ed. New York: George R. Lockwood and Son, 1886.

Brown, Sterling A., Arthur P. Davis, and Ulysses Lee. *The Negro Caravan*. New York: Citadel Press, 1941.

Carter, Roland. Interviewed by Bernice Johnson Reagon, 1993. Audio recording and transcript, *Wade In the Water* collection, Smithsonian Institution, National Museum of American History, Archives Center.

Cieply, Peter. *Stagebill*. <*http://www.stagebill.com/theater/profilesarchive/ breuer.html*>.

Douglass, Frederick. *Narrative of the Life of Frederick Douglass, An American Slave: Written by Himself*. Anti-Slavery Office, 1845. Reprint, New York: Penguin, 1982.

Du Bois, William Edward Burghardt. *Black Reconstruction in America, 1860– 1880*. 1935. Reprint, New York: Meridian Books, 1967.

————. *The Souls of Black Folk*. 1903. Reprint, New York: Knopf, 1993.

Epstein, Dena. *Sinful Tunes and Spirituals*. Urbana: University of Illinois Press, 1970.

Foner, Philip. *Paul Robeson Speaks*. New York: Citadel Press, 1978.

Gilbert, Olive. *The Narrative of Sojourner Truth*. 1950. Reprint, New York: Oxford University Press, 1991.

Harris, McCree. Interviewed by Jesse Johnson Jr., March 1996, Albany GA. Bernice Johnson Reagon Archives, Washington DC.

Harris, Michael W. "Conflict and Resolution in the Life of Thomas Andrew Dorsey." In Reagon, *We'll Understand It Better By and By*.

————. *Rise of Gospel Blues: The Music of Thomas Andrew Dorsey in the Urban Church*. New York: Oxford University Press, 1992.

Hayes, Roland. *My Songs: Afraamerican Religious Folk Songs Arranged and Interpreted by Roland Hayes*. Boston: Little, Brown, 1948.

Jackson, George Pullen. *White Spirituals in Southern Uplands*. Chapel Hill: University of North Carolina Press, 1933.

Johnson, James Weldon, and J. Rosamond Johnson. *The Book of American Negro Spirituals*. New York: Viking Press, 1925.

———. *The Books of American Negro Spirituals: Two Volumes in One*. Viking Press, 1940; reprint, New York: DaCapo Press, n.d.

Johnson, Jesse. Recorded audio statement by author, March 1996, Atlanta GA. Bernice Johnson Reagon Archives, Washington DC.

Jones, Bessie. *For the Ancestors: Autobiographical Memories*. Ed. John Stewart. Urbana: University of Illinois Press, 1992.

Jones, Bessie, and Bess Lomax Hawes. *Step It Down: Games, Plays, Songs and Stories from the Afro-American Heritage*. New York: Harper and Row, 1972.

Jones, Ralph. *Charles Albert Tindley, Prince of Preachers*. Nashville: Abingdon Press, 1982.

Logan, Rayford. *The Betrayal of the Negro*. London: Collier Books, 1965.

Mabee, Carlton, and Susan Mabee Newhouse. *Sojourner Truth: Slave, Prophet, Legend*. New York: New York University Press, 1993.

National Public Radio and the Smithsonian Institution. *Wade in the Water: African American Sacred Music Traditions*. Radio series, 1994.

Nierenberg, George T. *Say Amen, Somebody*. Film. GTN Productions, 1983.

Painter, Nell Irwin. *Exodusters: Black Migration to Kansas After Reconstruction*. New York: Knopf, 1976.

———. *Sojourner Truth: A Life, a Symbol*. New York: Norton, 1996.

———. "Soul Murder and Slavery: Toward a Fully Loaded Cost Accounting." In *U.S. History as Women's History: New Feminist Essays*. Ed. Linda K. Kerber, Alice Kessler-Harris, and Kathryn Kish Sklar. Chapel Hill: University of North Carolina Press, 1991.

Reagon, Bernice Johnson. "The Evolution of a Freedom Song, 'We Shall

Overcome.' " In *Songs of the Civil Rights Movement, 1955–1965: A Study in Culture History*. Ph.D. dissertation, Howard University, 1975.

———. "Kenneth Morris: 'I'll Be a Servant for the Lord.' " In Reagon, *We'll Understand It Better By and By*.

———. Program notes for "A Program of Spirituals." Performed by Kathleen Battle and Jessye Norman, Carnegie Hall, New York, March 18, 1990. *Stagebill, Carnegie Hall*. New York: Carnegie Hall, 1990.

———. "Searching for Tindley." In Reagon, *We'll Understand It Better By and By*.

Reagon, Bernice Johnson, ed. *We'll Understand It Better By and By: Pioneering African American Gospel Composers*. Washington DC: Smithsonian Press, 1992.

Reardon, William. Series of interviews by Bernice Johnson Reagon, 1986–93. Bernice Johnson Reagon Archives, Washington DC.

Robeson, Paul. *The Spectator*. London, June 15, 1934. In Foner, *Paul Robeson Speaks*.

Searles, Arthur C. Interviewed by Jesse Johnson Jr., March 1996, Albany GA. Bernice Johnson Reagon Archives, Washington DC.

Shockley, Ann Allen. "Fisk Jubilee Singers: Centennial Year, 1871–1971." In *BANG!* 2:48. Special Collections, Fisk University Library, Nashville.

Smallwood, Richard. *Adoration: Richard Smallwood, Live in Atlanta with Vision*. Sound recording. Verity Records, 01241-43015-2, 1996.

———. Telephone interview by Bernice Johnson Reagon, July 22, 1999. Bernice Johnson Reagon Archives, Washington DC.

Southern, Eileen. *The Music of Black Americans: A History*. New York: Norton, 1971.

Still, William. *The Underground Railroad*. 1871. Reprint, Chicago: Johnson Publishing Co., Ebony Classics, 1970.

Truth, Sojourner. *Narrative of Sojourner Truth: A Bondswoman of Olden Time, with a History of Her Labors and Correspondence Drawn from Her "Book of*

Life". 1878. Reprint, New York: Oxford University Press, 1971.

Turner, Patricia. "Fisk Jubilee Singers." In *Dictionary of Afro-American Performers*. New York: Garland, 1989. 170–74.

Weise, Arthur Jones. *Troy's One Hundred Years*. Troy NY: Rensselaer County Historical Society, 1890.

Williams, Smallwood Edmond. *This Is My Story: A Significant Life Struggle*. Washington DC: Wm. Willoughby Publishers, 1981.

Williams-Jones, Pearl. "Afro-American Gospel Music: A Crystallization of the Black Aesthetic." *Journal of Ethnomusicology* 19.3 (Sept. 1975): 373–85.

———. "Roberta Martin: Spirit of an Era." In Reagon, *We'll Understand It Better By and By*.

———, and Bernice Johnson Reagon. "Conversations: Roberta Martin Singers Roundtable." In Reagon, *We'll Understand It Better By and By*.

Permissions

Lyrics from "Search Me Lord," "Walking Up the King's Highway," and "Precious Lord," by Thomas Dorsey, appear here by permission of Warner/Chappell Music, Inc.

Lyrics from "Juba," with new words and new music adaptation by Bessie Jones, collected and edited with additional new material by Alan Lomax, appear here by permission of The Richmond Organization – (c) Copyright 1967 (Renewed) Ludlow Music, Inc., New York NY.

Lyrics from "Rollin' Under (Reg'lar, Reg'lar)," collected and adapted by Alan Lomax, appear here by permission of The Richmond Organization – (c) Copyright 1966 (Renewed) Ludlow Music, Inc.

Lyrics from "God Is Still on the Throne," by Roberta Martin, appear here by permission of Leonard Austin.

Lyrics from "Total Praise," by Richard Smallwood, appear here by permission of Richard Smallwood.

In the
ABRAHAM LINCOLN
LECTURE SERIES

Sander L. Gilman
*Smart Jews: The Construction of the Image of
Jewish Superior Intelligence*

Gerald Vizenor
*Fugitive Poses: Native American Indian Scenes of
Absence and Presence*

Linda Hutcheon and Michael Hutcheon
Bodily Charm: Living Opera

Bernice Johnson Reagon
*If You Don't Go, Don't Hinder Me: The African
American Sacred Song Tradition*